BIG LESSONS
COME IN
SMALL
PACKAGES

THINGS WE LEARN
FROM THE CATS WE LOVE

Inspired by Faith

Big Lessons Come In Small Packages
©Product Concept Mfg., Inc.

Big Lessons Come In Small Packages
ISBN 978-0-9963868-7-6

Published by Product Concept Mfg., Inc.
2175 N. Academy Circle #200, Colorado Springs, CO 80909

Written and Compiled by Eva Allen
in association with Product Concept Mfg., Inc.

All scripture quotations are from the King James version
of the Bible unless otherwise noted.

Scriptures taken from the Holy Bible,
New International Version®, NIV®.
Copyright © 1973, 1978, 1984 by Biblica, Inc.™
Used by permission of Zondervan.
All rights reserved worldwide.
www.zondervan.com

Sayings not having a credit listed are contributed by writers
for Product Concept Mfg., Inc. or in a rare case,
the author is unknown.

BIG LESSONS

COME IN

SMALL
PACKAGES

A little drowsing cat
   is an image of perfect beatitude.

Jules Champfleury

When you need a little inspiration in life, pay attention to a cat.

Cats have so many things to teach us... about enjoying a patch of sunlight, sacrificing for others, learning to trust, being alert and taking action, and above all, unconditional love.

These stories of kittens who are mischievous, funny, and smart; and cats who are shy, brave, and loving, are sure to warm your heart, lift your spirits, and bless your day... especially when you enjoy them in the company of a good cat!

THE HEALING IS MUTUAL

Animals are such agreeable friends—
they ask no questions; they pass no criticisms.

George Eliot

I looked up as the young man entered the animal shelter.
He was tall, with good posture, and a buzzcut hair style. He
seemed a bit uncertain as he approached the counter.

"Hello," I said. "Is there something I can help you with?"

"Yes, ma'am," he responded. "I would like to adopt a cat."

"Wonderful! If you wouldn't mind filling out this
application first, we can go look at the available kitties."

A few minutes later, we were heading toward the cat room.
The young man's name was Justin, I had learned from reading
his application form, and he had listed no current
employment information.

"Are you between jobs?" I asked, partly to be conversa-
tional and partly to assure myself that he could afford to take
care of a cat.

"Yes, ma'am, I guess that's what you could call it. I was in
the Marines and did three tours of duty in Iraq. But ever since
I left the service, I've had trouble keeping a job. Some days

I was just too depressed to get out of bed and go to work. Or if I did go, I might end up in an argument with one of my co-workers. I've been having a lot of nightmares and flash-backs. Finally, I was diagnosed with PTSD – you know, Post Traumatic Stress Disorder. I'm on disability right now."

"I'm sorry to hear you are going through all that," I said, "especially after serving our country so bravely."

"Thank you, ma'am," he said, "but 'bravely' may not be the best word for it." He grinned. "Anyway the reason I am here to adopt a cat is that my therapist thought it would be helpful for me to have one."

"Well, they say that just petting a kitty can lower your blood pressure. Have you had pets before?"

"Yes, ma'am. We had both dogs and cats when I was growing up, but I haven't had a pet as an adult."

Justin and I entered the cat room, which is a much cheerier place than many people expect it to be. Most of the cats roam free, with food, water, and various sleeping options available. The walls are painted happy colors, and the shelves and boxes are usually filled with dozing felines.

The friendliest of the cats immediately ran up to meet the two of us, arching their backs as they rubbed against our legs. Justin sat down on the floor and was soon overrun with kitties, including a few who tried to climb up onto his shoulder.

"As you can see," I said, "we have lots of cats to choose from. Or if you are interested in a kitten, we have them in another room."

"No, ma'am, I think I prefer an adult cat," he said. "One that's seen a little bit of the rougher side of life might be a good match for me."

"Well, we have those, too, I'm sorry to say. Stray cats, abused cats, abandoned cats, cats who have been hit by cars – the list goes on and on."

Justin nodded. "Isn't it hard for you to work here, seeing what people do to animals?"

"Yes, sometimes it is," I admitted, "but I also see what happens after animals are taken in and given proper care. And when they get adopted, that's the best part of all."

"Well, I hope I can make that happen for one kitty, at least." Justin gently pushed the cats off his lap and stood up. He walked around the room, looking at the cats who had stayed in their beds or cubbyholes. Finally, he stopped, studying a little gray tabby who watched us warily from her perch on a shelf. "Who's this one?" he asked.

"That's Mindy," I told him. "She came to us from a hoarding situation, and she's very shy. She's been here almost two years."

"Two years!"

"Yes, unfortunately, some cats just don't seem to get picked by adopters. People tend to like cats who are more friendly and outgoing. Mindy responds to some of the volunteers who have been coming here for a while, but she's leery of strangers."

Justin slowly extended a hand toward the cat. "Hello there," he said softly. "I'm not going to hurt you."

I expected Mindy to retreat from him, but to my surprise, she didn't. In fact, after a moment, she stretched forward to sniff Justin's fingers. Then, ever so slowly, she began to move toward him while he continued to talk quietly to her. In an amazingly short time, he was stroking her chin and ears.

"I can't believe it!" I said. "She really seems to like you."

"I like her, too," Justin said. "I think she's the one I want to adopt."

I warned him that Mindy might be totally freaked out by the move to his house, and spend some time in hiding during the first few days.

"I can be patient with her, if she can be patient with me," he responded with a smile.

So that's how Justin, the ex-Marine, adopted Mindy, the little tabby cat—both suffering from traumatic experiences and ready to help each other heal.

I kept in touch with Justin just to find out how he and Mindy were doing. He told me that it had taken a couple of days for the kitty to start eating more than a mouthful or two at meals. But before long, she got used to Justin and his schedule. She began sitting in his lap while he watched TV or used the computer. At night, she curled up next to him on the bed.

A few months after the adoption, Justin stopped by the shelter to chat. He told me that he had found some work he could do from home, on his own schedule. Also, he was earning money by taking care of cats while their owners were out of town.

Justin was experiencing fewer nightmares, but when he did have one, he could take comfort in having Mindy close by, purring and wanting to be petted. And sometimes the cat had even awakened him just as a bad dream was starting, as if she knew it should be avoided.

"I can't thank you enough for letting me adopt her," Justin concluded. " I had no idea it would make such a difference in my life."

"You've made a huge difference in Mindy's life, too," I reminded him. "If it weren't for you, she might have never experienced having a home of her own."

And there were tears in my eyes as I gave him a hug.

IN GIVING, WE RECEIVE

You have not lived today until you have done
something for someone who can never repay you.
John Bunyan

The subject of the sermon had been serving others. The pastor said that if we look around, we can always find some way to help someone else in need. He ended by reminding us that the real service begins after we leave the worship service.

I thought about this while I was driving home from church. I was 72 years old, retired, widowed, and on a fixed income. I was also somewhat overweight and I had bad knees. After I first retired, I volunteered several times a week at the local children's hospital. I reluctantly gave that up because of my knees, but I am still quite active in the women's group at church. We make quilts for families that need them. In addition, I knit little caps for newborns in third-world countries.

So when it comes to service, I feel that I have done, and continue to do, a reasonable amount. However, I couldn't quite get the minister's words out of my head.

After I ate some lunch, I turned on my computer to check my email. One of the posts in my neighborhood discussion list particularly caught my attention. A woman named Debbie was asking for recommendations for a cat sitter. An older friend of Debbie's was in rehab because of a badly broken leg. Someone was needed to feed the cat once a day so that he could stay in his house rather than being boarded.

When I read this, I got excited. Here was a way I could serve. I felt as if I were actually being called to help out in this situation. I sent a private message to Debbie and offered to take care of her friend's cat for free. I told her I had owned many cats over the years and still had one, along with two chihuahuas.

Debbie called me within the hour. I admitted that I was not a professional cat sitter, but I gave her the names of my veterinarian and my minister as references.

"I know how it is, getting older," I told her. "We all start needing more help. That's why I would be happy to help your friend and her cat."

The next day I went to meet LeRoy, the cat in question. He was orange and white, an older fellow who had lost some weight during the week or so he had been boarded at his vet's office. He was very talkative and enjoyed being loved on. He and I hit it off right away.

Every afternoon I went to LeRoy's house, fed him, scooped out the litter box, and then just sat with him for a while. Sometimes I took along a book to read, and sometimes I watched TV. LeRoy didn't care what I did; he just liked having the company.

Debbie gave me her friend Helen's phone number at the rehab center, so I called. We talked at some length about LeRoy, about her broken leg, about her previous career as an artist. She told me she was feeling pretty bored there, which led me to start visiting her a couple of times a week. She turned out to be quite an interesting person, and I really enjoyed talking to her.

After six weeks, Helen got to come home. LeRoy was delighted to see her, of course. I still visit Helen on a regular basis. Sometimes she and Debbie and I go out to see a movie and to dinner together.

I never dreamed, when I responded to that request for a cat sitter, that I would end up with two wonderful new friends, but that's how it worked out. "Give, and it shall be given unto you," the Bible tells us in Luke 6:38. How could I have forgotten that?

GRACIE

What greater gift than the love of a cat?
Charles Dickens

I had been working at the skilled nursing care facility for a couple of years before Gracie joined our staff. She has always been so pleasant to have around, never grumpy or out-of-sorts. I've really learned a lot from her, and I consider her to be one of the best co-workers I've ever had.

Many times, while I am on the night shift, I see Gracie making her rounds. She moves softly along the hallways, stopping at each room to be certain that its occupants are resting peacefully.

If she comes upon any patients who are awake and fretful, Gracie always takes time to sit quietly beside them for a while. It's amazing how much comfort folks seem to draw from Gracie's presence. She has such a wonderful gift for calming the restless spirit.

Gracie often works the day shift, too. I can't tell you how many times I've seen her bring a smile to a patient's face. Sometimes she can even elicit a response from dementia patients who have long ago retreated into their own private worlds.

The whole staff loves Gracie. She always seems to know how to cheer us up when we are feeling stressed or sad. Having her around is just a very special blessing.

Oh, and maybe I should mention that Gracie is a cat. She is quite beautiful – mostly white, with some gray tabby spots. We're not sure where she came from. One day she just showed up at the back door when deliveries were being made for the kitchen. The chef gave her a little tuna and then tried to get one of us to take her to the local shelter. Of course, no one wanted to, fearing that she would be euthanized.

Finally, the chaplain volunteered to keep Gracie in his office until something could be found to do with her. In the meantime, he began to take Gracie around with him when he visited some of the patients.

She was quite a hit with them, and soon they were asking to see her often. That is how she ended up becoming a permanent part of our staff. We never did figure out where Gracie came from or how she ended up at our door. She was simply a gift to us – much like the gift of Grace, which is given freely and which is meant to be accepted in the same way.

RETURNING THE FAVOR

Arise from sleep, old cat,
And with great yawns and stretchings...
Amble out for love.

Japanese Haiku, Kobayashi Issa

My wife had always had an unfortunate desire to feed every stray animal that came anywhere near our house. So that meant a pack of feral cats was usually hanging around at dinnertime, waiting for a handout, along with a few possums and even the occasional raccoon.

But mostly it was cats, which led to our spending a lot of money on kibble, vaccinations and neutering. In my opinion, those funds could have been better spent on movies or eating out. But Mary is my wife and I love her, so I humor her on this.

Luckily, because the cats we were feeding were feral, they had no desire to come into our house. Mary would have gone to the local shelter to adopt a bunch of tame cats to live with us, but that's where I drew the line. We were already spending a fortune on the outside cats, and our salaries could only go so far. Besides which, I'm not a big fan of cat hair. So Mary humored me on that, and we got along fine.

But one evening I arrived home from work late and found a big, bedraggled-looking gray cat eating from a dish in the middle of the kitchen floor. Mary was watching him, looking pleased as punch.

"Okay, what's going on here?" I asked.

"This is Oscar," Mary replied. "He was just sitting on the back steps, and when I opened the door, he marched right in and made himself at home."

"You mean that you made him at home by giving him some food."

"Well, that helped," she admitted with a smile.

"How do you know his name is Oscar?"

"He just looks like an Oscar, don't you think?"

I shrugged. "Maybe. I'm not sure what an Oscar looks like."

"Well, this is an old, grouchy cat who has seen better days, I think," Mary said. "His coat is all rough and patchy, and he walks with sort of a limp. I'm guessing he may have some arthritis."

"So what do you plan to do with him?"

"I'll try to find his owner first, of course," she said. "I think he must have belonged to somebody, or else he wouldn't have just walked into the house like that."

"And if you don't find the owner?"

"Well, I was hoping maybe we could keep him."

"You know how I feel about having cats living in the house, Honey."

"Yes, but Oscar is an old guy who just needs a warm, safe place to live out the rest of his life."

"Old cats can be expensive because of all their health problems," I reminded her.

"I know, but let me just try to find his owner first, and then we can talk about it."

"All right," I sighed.

But I knew how it would be, and that's the way it was. Mary did make a good-faith effort to find Oscar's owner, but the cat was not microchipped, and there were no responses to her ads or posters.

After she decided that we had spent enough time looking for the former owner, Mary took Oscar to the veterinarian for an exam, vaccinations, and neutering. Poor old guy, I guess he never bargained on all of that the day he first walked into our kitchen. And I never bargained on how much it was going to cost. But Mary was happy, and I suppose that made it all worthwhile.

Oscar wasn't a very exciting cat to have around. Mostly, he just ate and slept. His arthritis kept him from jumping up on things, so he didn't get into any mischief. At night he curled up in a deep, soft cat bed in the corner of our bedroom. Mary had wanted to buy one of those little staircases that people have so their chihuahuas can climb on their beds, but I said no.

The months went by, and I got used to having a cat in the house. Of course, Oscar was such a low-profile sort of guy that I tended to forget he was even around. Sometimes Mary lifted him into her lap when we were sitting around in the evening, watching TV. He lay there and purred and eventually went to sleep. He pretty much ignored me, though, and I returned the favor.

Christmastime came, and Mary decorated in her usual effusive way, with the hundreds of ornaments and lights she had collected over the years. This was another thing in which I humored her. I liked to see her happy, and decorating for holidays so we could entertain our kids and grandkids always made Mary happy.

On Christmas Eve, after all the presents had been opened, the meal had been eaten, and all our guests had gone home, Mary and I fell into bed, completely exhausted. I'm not sure how long we had been sleeping when I was halfway wakened by the sound of loud meowing and frantic scratching at my side of the bed.

"Quit it, Oscar!" I mumbled. "It's not time for breakfast!" Oscar didn't quit, so I elbowed Mary. "Go see what's wrong with your cat," I told her.

But she continued snoring. I sat up in bed, and was suddenly wide awake. The acrid smell of smoke was heavy in the air, and the nightlight was just a fuzzy blur out in the hall.

"Mary!" I cried, shaking her hard. "Wake up! We've got to get out! The house is on fire!"

"Oh, Lord help us!" she exclaimed as she sat up and clambered out of bed. "Where's Oscar?"

But I was already on my hands and knees, feeling underneath the bed. As soon as my hand contacted his furry body, I hauled him out, yowling.

"Got him! Let's go!"

The smoke was so thick that we could barely breathe, and we had to feel our way along the hall. The living room was totally ablaze.

"The Christmas tree lights!" Mary exclaimed. "I forgot to unplug them!" She was coughing hard by then, and so was I.

"This way," I said, pushing her toward the kitchen. We stumbled through the smoke to the back door and out into the yard. Then, in our pajamas, barefooted, and with me still clutching Oscar, we headed next door to call the fire department.

Our house wasn't a total loss, but we did have to move out for several months. I insisted we find a place that would allow Oscar to be with us. "We have to take good care of him," I told Mary. "After all, he saved our lives."

"Yes, he did," she responded, and smiled that knowing smile of hers.

THANK YOU TO MY WONDERFUL CAT

For all the times you've greeted me
at the door with your tail waving happily...

And for every time you've jumped
in my lap and purred my worries away...

For entertaining me with your playful antics...

And for rubbing against me
and doing your silly head-butting...

For lending me your warm,
snuggly presence on cold nights...

And for listening to me so patiently
when I really need to talk...

For adopting me, teaching me love...

And for bringing such joy to my life!

A CAT THAT OPENS DOORS

Intelligence in cats is underrated.
Louis Wain

When the company I worked for went bankrupt, I couldn't find another job that paid as much as I was previously earning. This meant that, unfortunately, I had to sell my house and move with my ten-year-old son Gavin to an apartment.

We found a place we liked in a nice neighborhood, but the location meant that Gavin had to change schools. Luckily, the apartment allowed pets, so we were able to take Hercules, my son's big yellow tabby cat with us.

Herc had been a birthday gift when Gavin turned eight. A lot of kids want ponies for their birthdays or for Christmas, but Gavin wanted a kitten. He had begged and pleaded for one for so long that I finally gave in and took him to the local shelter to pick one out.

Gavin chose the friendly little fur ball that later grew up to be big, mellow Hercules. I can tell you for a fact that that cat never met anybody he didn't like. However, his ultimate devotion was to Gavin, and the boy felt the same about his feline pal.

The move to the new neighborhood and the change of schools were pretty hard on my son. He had always been a quiet boy, but now he became alarmingly withdrawn. I don't know what secrets and tears Gavin shared with Hercules, but there must have been many. I do know that my son started spending a lot of hours in his room, reading, doing homework, listening to music, and pouring his heart out to Herc.

I had feared that my son's grades might suffer during this period of transition, but they didn't. The biggest problem was that Gavin didn't seem to have any friends—well, besides his cat, of course.

"Would you like to ask somebody to go to the movies with you?" I inquired on more than one occasion.

But the answer was always, "No, not really."

"What's going on?" I prodded. "You don't seem to have any friends. Aren't there any nice kids in your new class?"

"I don't know. Maybe a few."

"Well, have you tried to talk to them?"

"I did in the beginning," he admitted, "but then they started making fun of me."

"Making fun of you? How?" And suddenly I felt very guilty that we hadn't had this conversation some weeks ago.

"Um, well, they call me a nerd and a wiseguy and a know-it-all. But I'm not!" he added quickly. "I'm not any of those things! I just get good grades because I study a lot."

"I know, Sweetie," I said, going to him and giving him a hug. "You're smart, and you learn quickly. That's nothing to be ashamed of."

"But what good does it do to be smart if you can't have any friends?" Gavin demanded. "And another thing they call me is a wimp because I'm not good at sports. And then when I told them I have a cat, a bunch of the boys laughed at me. They all have dogs. They said that only sissies have cats."

I sighed and hugged him again. He was crying by now, and I was wishing I knew some way to take away his pain. It wasn't until later that night, while I was lying wide awake in bed, that I came up with an idea that I thought might work.

The next morning was Saturday, and at the breakfast table, I said to Gavin, "You know, cats can be trained to do tricks, just like dogs can."

"You're kidding."

"No, I'm not."

"What kinds of tricks?"

"Well, I'm not sure about all the things they can do, but I

have heard of cats jumping through hoops and doing agility training, sort of like dogs do."

"Agility?" he asked. "What's that?"

"Go look it up," I suggested. "And look for 'cat tricks' online. Maybe you can teach Herc some tricks, and then you can have him perform for those kids who think you're a sissy because you have a cat."

Gavin gave me a look of disbelief, but he trotted off to his bedroom. He came back with his laptop, which he opened up and typed in a search. Soon he was watching videos of cats performing all sorts of tricks.

"Mom, you won't believe what some of these cats can do!" he exclaimed. "Come look!"

So we watched the videos together, including a few on positive training methods using a clicker.

"Do you think Herc could learn some tricks?" Gavin asked. "A couple of the sites say you should start training your cat when he's still a kitten. Herc is already two years old!"

"You know what? I don't think that will matter. Hercules is such a smart kitty that he won't have any trouble learning tricks. He's already taught himself to open the kitchen cabinet doors."

Gavin laughed. "Okay, I want to try teaching him.

Can we go to the pet store and buy a clicker and a tunnel and maybe a few other things?"

For the next few weeks, my son and his big yellow cat spent all their spare time training. Soon they had an impressive routine worked up. It included doing some high-fives, sitting, rolling over, jumping through a hoop, running through a tunnel, and fetching a ball.

When Gavin felt that Hercules was good enough at doing his tricks, the boy signed up for a talent show that his class was having. I took a day off from work so that I could watch the performance. Also, I needed to take Herc home when it was over.

I'll admit that I was a nervous wreck. I was so afraid that Gavin's cat would not perform in front of an audience— especially one that contained members who were skeptical, to say the least. All I could do was pray that the big kitty would come through for the boy who loved him so much.

And come through he did. Hercules seemed a bit distracted when he was first called on to do a trick, but Gavin patiently asked the cat to focus on him, then gave the command again. From then on, it was smooth sailing. The other members of the class soon fell silent and watched in amazement. Enthusiastic applause followed the act.

"Did anybody say anything to you about Hercules after I left?" I asked Gavin that afternoon. I was sitting in my favorite chair, trying to read with a big yellow cat on my lap.

"Yeah, a lot of people told me they liked it." He was beaming. "And some of those boys – the ones who made fun of me because I have a cat – they said they didn't know cats could be that smart."

"Well, I guess you proved something to them."

"Yeah. Oh, and Tyler, this guy who does a lot of skateboarding, asked if I could teach Herc to ride a skateboard. So I told him I'd try. Tyler's going to help me."

"I'll have to make a video of that," I said, "and we can post it online."

"That would be great," Gavin said, as he headed for his room.

Then Hercules gave a little "Mmrph" sound, jumped down, and followed him.

I sat there still smiling, thinking about what Hercules had just taught us. That sometimes a cat can be a boy's best friend. Their special bond between boy and cat broke barriers, opening the door to new experiences and friendships.

PLAYING FAVORITES

The smallest feline is a masterpiece.
Leonardo da Vinci

In my studied opinion, everyone needs a cat like my little Martha. She is my most adventuresome, curious, cuddly, insistent, loving, annoying, and favorite cat. I have two other cats, and I love them both dearly, but something about Martha has grabbed hold of my heart in a very special way.

When I first became Martha's foster mom, she had two kittens. A woman surrendered the little feline family at the local shelter because she could no longer take care of them. She had lost her home to foreclosure and was living in her car. There were four kittens in the beginning, but the woman had managed to find homes for two.

So I brought the little homeless mama and her kittens to my house. I named her Martha, and I called the two female kittens Mimi and Mouse.

Martha is such a petite cat that it's hard to imagine her giving birth to four kittens. She has sleek black fur, a lovely white star on her chest, and luminous gold eyes. She weighs in at about six pounds.

Almost as soon as the gray tabby kittens had been spayed, they were adopted by a family with twin boys.

In the meantime, Martha explored the house thoroughly, slipping behind and under furniture, through crevices, and leaping onto tall chests of drawers.

Martha's very favorite place is the basement. I only allow the cats to go down there when I am doing laundry, but Martha always makes the most of the opportunity. She reconnoiters rafters, ductwork, and the top of foundation walls. She emerges with cobwebs all over her whiskers and ears. It seems that she can go places where there are no places to go!

One day I left the basement door open so that Martha could finish her investigations while I took my shower. She came upstairs later and curled up in one of the cat beds. I became concerned at suppertime, when she didn't show up to eat. I fed the other cats and then went looking for Martha.

She was still in the cat bed, and when I started petting her, I realized she had an alarming injury on the side of her face. My best guess was that she had burned herself on a hot water pipe in the basement while I was showering.

Luckily, it was still ten minutes before time for the vet's office to close. I called them and then hurried over there with Martha. The vet agreed that the cat had likely burned herself. After a couple of weeks on antibiotics, she healed up nicely, and when the fur grew back in, it was impossible to tell that anything had happened.

After Martha was spayed, we posted photos and a description of her online. On Saturdays, I took her to adoption events, but she did not "show well," huddling in her cage and not letting anyone see what a loving, sweet kitty she was at home. Plus it seemed that she was always overlooked in favor of kittens or cats who were not mostly black.

Meanwhile, I started noticing that whenever Martha jumped up onto something – which was frequently – she tended to drag one hind leg a little bit. The rescue group okayed the funds for an x-ray, and we learned that Martha had hip dysplasia.

Dogs often suffer from this condition, but it's pretty unusual for a cat to have it. In hip dysplasia, which is a genetic condition, the ball at the top of the thigh bone does not fit properly into the socket. This, in turn, means that the hip joint may not function smoothly. That's a somewhat simplistic explanation, but suffice it to say that I worried about Martha's needing expensive surgery or eventually becoming severely arthritic.

Then I found a veterinary orthopedist who offered to do a free consultation. He looked at Martha's x-rays, flexed her hip joints, and told me that he doubted the dysplasia would ever cause Martha any real problems.

Not long after that, I decided to adopt Martha myself. Yes, I'm a sucker, but the little cat had totally wormed her way into my heart. My other two cats tolerate her, and she returns the favor. Martha never snuggles with them, but she is aggressively affectionate with me. Even on the hottest night, I can rely on her to be ensconced in my armpit or against my body.

She is an excellent alarm clock, too. Every morning at 6:00 or 6:30, she begins to walk back and forth across me, no matter how many times I shove her off and mumble, "Seven o'clock. Come back at seven!"

Martha has broken two of my principal rules: No Cats on the Kitchen Counter and No Cats on the Dining Room Table. She has broken these rules so repeatedly that I finally gave up trying to enforce them. Now I just feel lucky if I can keep her from stealing a mouthful of tuna casserole right off my plate.

So that's the story of Martha – how I fostered her, fell in love with her, adopted her, and learned a lot from her. Sometimes she frustrates me, but more often she makes me laugh. She's a very small cat with a very big heart. She has taught me so much about curiosity, persistence, gracefulness, and beauty. And most of all, she has taught me so much about love.

FINDING MR. RIGHT

Beware of people who dislike cats.

Proverb

I give my Persian cat Henrietta full credit for the fact that I am now married to the most wonderful man in the world.

Some people start their search for a life partner with the guideline "must like dogs," but mine was "must like cats." More specifically, it was "must like Henrietta" (who was not always the most likeable of cats) and finally, "must be liked *by* Henrietta." The last was a hurdle that very few men could hope to clear.

I was too leery of online dating services to try that approach, so I mostly met potential dates at my church-sponsored singles group, or I went out with men that friends and co-workers suggested I would like.

Many of these encounters didn't get beyond my asking my date whether he had any pets. Men who deemed themselves too busy to have a pet or who were allergic to cats or who liked only dogs were instantly eliminated from consideration.

Men who said they liked cats and whose company I enjoyed were brought home to meet Henrietta. If she hissed and growled at them when they attempted to pet her, it was game over. I considered Henrietta to be an excellent judge of character, and I knew I could learn a lot from her. I was not going to marry someone she didn't like.

I first met John when a friend set me up with him. We got together at a little coffee shop a few blocks from my house. He was tall and wore thick glasses that made him look a bit nerdish. But he seemed kind, and he had the most beautiful green eyes. When he smiled at me with those eyes, I felt as if a window had opened that let me see all the way into his soul. And I really liked what I saw.

John did not have any pets at the time I met him; his apartment building did not allow them. But he told me he had grown up with cats. In fact, his parents still had one.

When John came to my place for the first time, I was pretty nervous. I already liked him quite a bit, and I really wanted Henrietta to like him, too. As he took a seat on the sofa, I apologized for the fact that it was spring, and thus the height of shedding season.

"I brush Henrietta every day," I said, "but some days you can't even tell I've done it."

"Don't worry," John replied with a grin. "I'll just wear light-colored clothes next time I come visit."

That was when Henrietta sauntered over to check out my date. She sniffed his shoes and pants legs with great interest, then hopped up on the sofa and sniffed in the direction of John's face. "Hello, pretty girl," he said. He reached out to scratch her gently under the chin, then stroked her back.

Henrietta's tail rose in a graceful curve as she walked onto John's lap. After a moment, she settled down there and began to purr. She looked at me through contented, half-closed eyes as if to say, "Finally, you found the right one!"

3-LEGGED INSPIRATION

God made the cat to give man
the pleasure of stroking a tiger.

Joseph Méry

The town where we live is not big enough to have a zoo, so our son Noah was almost six years old when we first took him to a big-city zoo. He was enthralled. He dragged us eagerly from one exhibit to the next, demanding that we read all the signs to him.

The big cats were Noah's favorites. And when he discovered a tiger with a missing leg, he was beside himself with curiosity.

"Daddy! Daddy!" he cried, tugging at my husband's arm. "Why does the tiger only have three legs? Does it say on the sign?"

"Well, let's see," Michael mused. "It says that this tiger got her leg caught in a trap when she was just a young cub. The doctors in Malaysia had to cut her leg off in order to save her life."

"She couldn't live in the wild with only three legs," I told Noah, "because she wouldn't be able to catch food to eat. So that's why she has been living in zoos."

"Are there doctors at this zoo, too?" Noah asked.

"Yes," Michael told him. "They're called veterinarians. I'll bet there are a lot of them here because there are so many animals to take care of."

"That's what I want to be," Noah announced. "A zoo veterinarian."

"There are other types of veterinarians," I said. "Some just take care of people's dogs and cats."

"Nope, I want to take care of tigers and elephants and giraffes," Noah insisted. "I want to be like Noah in the Bible. He built a great big ark and put all the animals on it and saved them from the flood."

"Well, if that's what you want to do, I'm sure you'll find a way to do it," Michael said. "But right now, I think we should have some lunch!"

A few weeks after that, my Aunt Jean called me to say that she was going to have to move into assisted living. "They won't let me take my cat," she said, and I could tell she was crying. "Can you help me find a home for him?"

"Of course we can," I assured her. "In fact, we will just adopt him ourselves!" I promised this without even consulting Michael or Noah, but I was certain they would feel the same way I did.

When we went to get the cat, we found a lanky orange tabby who was missing one of his front legs.

"Mommy!" Noah exclaimed. "This cat is just like the tiger in the zoo! Can we name him Tiger?"

"This cat already has a name," I told him.

Aunt Jean laughed. "His name is Maximilian," she said, "but you can change it if you want to."

So Maximilian became Tiger, and he lived a long, happy life with us. Noah learned so much from that cat, both about felines and about animals in general. He read everything he could find on tigers and jaguars and all the big cats, as well as many other exotic animals.

On the day Noah got his degree in veterinary science, I couldn't help thinking of that first day we had taken him to the zoo, and especially of the three-legged tiger we had seen there. And now, so many years later, my heart was overflowing with love and thanksgiving for this wonderful son of ours – this modern-day Noah who had made it his goal in life to save as many animals as he possibly could.

A DIFFERENT KIND OF TEACHER

Things do not change; we change.
Henry David Thoreau

I've always been a real go-getter type of guy – ambitious, competitive, and impatient. I drove myself hard to get top grades in school, finished college in three years, and went to work for a high-powered ad agency. Deadlines just goaded me on. I would do almost anything and put in any number of hours to meet them.

My wife Molly warned me that if I didn't slow down, there would be dire consequences to my health. But Molly is my wife and a nurse, so of course she would say that kind of thing.

Then at age 45, I had a heart attack. It didn't kill me, so I guess it could have been worse, but it definitely scared me into thinking about my life in a different way. I spent three days in the hospital after a stent was put in my coronary artery, and then came home feeling weak and bewildered.

It seemed as if everything about my life had changed. Suddenly I had to start taking a ton of pills every day. My diet now consisted of lots of boring vegetables and lean meat with no salt. And soon I would be expected to go out and take daily walks.

Worst of all, Molly absolutely insisted that I leave the ad agency. "That job will kill you if you don't quit it. You know I'm right!"

I did know she was right, but I wasn't ready to admit it. "What about my salary?" I asked her. "We can't just live on yours. And what will I do with myself? I can't sit around twiddling my thumbs all the time. I'll go nuts!"

"You're a good writer," she said. "You can do some freelancing. Or how about writing that novel you always talked about?"

"Humpf," I grumbled, unconvinced.

"Well, at least you should take it easy for a few weeks," Molly said. "You need time to get healed up and strong again."

The concept of "take it easy" was totally foreign to me, so when Molly started getting ready to leave for work the next day, I found myself feeling a bit panicky.

There is nothing like facing your own mortality to make you re-look your priorities. But I was wired a certain way.

"What am I supposed to do all day?" I demanded. "I'm used to having a big ad campaign to work on."

"Just take a few lessons from Chloe," Molly said. "She knows all about relaxing and enjoying life." Then with a merry wave, she headed out the door.

Chloe? Chloe, our cat? I honestly had never paid much attention to Chloe because I hadn't been home that much. What kinds of lessons could a cat possibly have to teach?

I wandered through the house until I found Chloe sleeping in a sunny spot on the living room carpet. I watched for a short time, but she wasn't really doing anything besides sleeping. Was that the lesson? Take a lot of naps?

Out on the deck, I discovered the weather to be quite pleasant. There was a nice breeze, and it wasn't too hot. I sat down in a lounge chair and tried to keep from worrying about how Molly and I could live on one salary and a little freelance money. It wasn't easy, but I managed to make myself relax a bit and focus on watching the birds at our feeder. Before I knew it, I had dozed off.

An hour later, I woke up, stretched, and went back inside, feeling surprisingly refreshed and much calmer. Chloe, I noticed, had followed the sunbeam to a new spot and was snoozing again.

I sat down at the computer to check my email, and after a short time, Chloe came over and hopped into my lap.

I took a photo of the two of us together, then signed onto my social network page. I posted the photo along with a message saying that I was being taken care of by my nurse, Chloe, while I recovered from my heart attack.

Almost immediately, I began getting positive responses and comments. People wished me a quick recovery, people said they were praying for me, people said that Chloe looked like a very competent nurse.

I was really moved by the outpouring of love and support. I barely knew some of these people, and yet they were concerned about me and were praying for me. Did this kind of thing happen all the time in online communities? I had never taken the time to find out.

Someone posted a link to a funny cat video, so I watched that. Then I watched another and another. I began to see how people could end up spending so much time on the internet. Quite a few of these people had jobs, I knew, but they were taking a few minutes out to connect with each other, to laugh, and to smell the virtual roses. Maybe I should have learned to do that.

After lunch, it occurred to me to take a look at the contents of our bookcase. When was the last time I had read a book? I honestly couldn't remember. Some of the titles were old friends, but there were many that were total strangers. Where had they come from? Had Molly bought them? Had I, thinking I would have time to read them someday? I picked out one that looked particularly interesting and sat down in the recliner.

Before I could even open the book, Chloe had jumped into my lap again. She was clearly delighted to have human company for the entire day. I stroked her soft fur, and she closed her eyes and purred. She began to knead my leg, very gently and rhythmically. I took a deep breath and let it out, releasing the tension that I did not even realize had been building up again.

"Yes, Chloe," I said, "I think you have a lot of fine lessons to teach me."

Then I opened the book and started reading.

MY CAT: A POEM

Blessed are those who love cats,
for they shall never be lonely.

Author Unknown

I have a cat whose name is Jill.
Her purring is a gentle trill.

She came to me one stormy night
When lightning streaked the sky with white.

She came to me; I let her in.
Her coat was wet, her body thin.

When she was dry and amply fed,
She curled up next to me in bed.

Could she have sensed that I'd been sad,
Or known what lonely days I'd had?

Was she the answer to my prayer?
She must have been, for she was there,

My little Jill so full of love,
Sent to me by God above.

SOMETHING LOST,
SOMETHING GAINED

Love is something eternal;
the aspect may change, but not the essence.
Vincent van Gogh

I had just finished vacuuming when I realized with a shock that my wedding ring was missing. It was just a simple gold band, but in the twenty-one years of my marriage to Sam, it had never once left my finger. Until now. I tried not to panic, but of course I did.

My mind frantically ran through all the places I had been in the last few hours, and all the things I had done. It would have helped if I knew how long the ring had been gone. How could I not have noticed it was missing? Why didn't I feel it slip off?

I began by searching all the nooks and crannies I had just vacuumed. I looked between sofa cushions, under furniture, along baseboards. I even took the sweeper bag out, slit it open and sifted through its contents. I did a lot of coughing and sneezing, but I did not find my ring.

Next I stuck my hand into the garbage disposal and felt around. The ring might have come off while I was washing a few dishes. But it wasn't there. Nor was it in the shower or anywhere else in the bathroom.

I stripped the bed and shook out all the bedclothes. I looked inside the pillow cases. I went out in the yard and raked through the dirt in my flower beds where I had been pulling weeds earlier. I looked in my car, pulling up the floor mats, shining a flashlight under all the seats and into the corners of the trunk.

Finally, exhausted, I dropped down in a chair and started crying. All I could think about was the day Sam had first put that ring on my finger as we exchanged our vows in front of the altar. Inside the ring, there was an inscription, now a bit worn and hard to read: Christy and Sam, In Love Forever. That ring meant so much to me, and now I had somehow stupidly lost it. I was still sitting there, moping, when Sam got home from work.

"What's wrong?" he asked immediately, with wary concern.

I got up and ran to him. "I lost my wedding ring!" I blurted out, and started crying all over again.

"Oh, Sweetheart," he said, and wrapped his strong arms around me. "Don't worry. It's only a ring."

"Only a ring?" I cried. "But it's my wedding ring!"

"Do you have to have a ring to feel like you're married, or to know how much I love you? I promised 'till death do us part,' and I still mean that, with or without a ring!"

I buried my face against his chest. "Oh, Sam, I love you so much. Thanks for being so sweet about this."

He smiled and hugged me again. "I'll help you look for the ring," he said, " and if we can't find it, I'll buy you another one."

"Can we afford another ring? The price of gold is so high, and now that I've quit my job, we only have your paycheck."

"We'll figure it out," he assured me. "I don't want my darling wife crying over a lost ring."

That evening Sam helped look for the ring, but although we searched everywhere we could think to look, we couldn't find it.

"Let's wait a couple of weeks." he said. "It may still show up."

The next day, I spent a few more hours searching the house, but without any luck.

That evening, when Sam came home from work, he brought a little black-and-white kitten.

"Oh, he's adorable!" I exclaimed, "or is it a she?"

"It's a he," Sam said. "One of the women in the office brought in a box of six kittens this morning. They were just dumped in the street in front of her house."

As I took the little creature in my hands, he began to produce a purr as loud as an outboard motor.

"Can we keep him?" I asked, laughing. But I already knew what the answer would be.

My worry about the lost wedding ring faded into the background as I started to focus on the needs of this tiny kitty, who was dependent on us for so much, yet who was already bringing so much delight into our lives.

That night we played with him until he wore us out. Then we sat down to watch TV. After a little while, I noticed that the kitten was carrying something around in his mouth. Then he would put it down and shove it around with his paw before picking it up again.

"Sam, could you go see what the kitten is playing with? We don't want him to swallow something that will choke him."

As soon as Sam approached him, the kitten scampered off with his treasure, but finally Sam caught up with him. As soon as he did, he started laughing.

"What is it? What's going on?" I asked.

Sam came over to my chair, holding the kitten in one hand. In his other outstretched palm, I saw the gold glint of my wedding band. My mind could barely register what I was seeing.

"Could he have possibly found it?" I murmured through happy tears as I slipped the ring back onto my finger.

"Who knows, but I'm thinking he's a real mystery-solver. Maybe we should name him Sherlock."

So Sherlock became the little guy's name. I was forever grateful to him for finding my ring. But I was even more grateful for being reminded that Sam's love for me was the real treasure. I really didn't need a ring to show me that.

LETTER TO THE EDITOR

Hi, my name is Troy, and I'm in the 5th grade. Last week my class went on a field trip to the animal shelter. When we got back, our teacher said we had to write a report or else a letter to the editor. I never wrote to an editor before, so I thought that would be more fun.

When we first got to the shelter, a lot of kids wanted to see the dogs, but I wanted to see the cats. I wish my family could have a cat, but my sister is allergic, so we can't. I got to play with the cats at the shelter and also brush them. The reason they are there is because they were strays or maybe their owners can't take care of them anymore. But it's not the cat's fault if it is in the shelter.

While we were there, some people adopted a cat. This made everyone very happy. I think more people need to go to the shelter and adopt cats and dogs. If you can't adopt one, you can at least go there and play with them. My mom said she would take me to the shelter sometimes on weekends so that I can play with the cats.

Maybe when I grow up, I can be a veterinarian and help a lot of animals who are sick or hurt. But even if I don't become a veterinarian, I for sure want to have a cat. And maybe a dog, too.

Well, thanks for reading my letter about the shelter. I know it's kind of long, but I hope you will print it anyway. I want everybody to know about the shelter and about how they should go there to adopt a dog or cat. Or at least volunteer!

Sincerely,
Troy

A NEW WAY OF SEEING

*A cat's eyes are windows
enabling us to see into another world.*

Proverb

None of us knew where the scruffy, scrawny kitten had come from or what she had been through before Animal Control picked her up. What was totally clear, though, was that she had a painful infection in both eyes.

The kitten, who was soon dubbed Marlee, got the best care the veterinary staff could offer, but she still ended up losing one eye. After her surgery, I brought her to my house for fostering and healing.

Marlee settled in pretty well to the general routine. But although she and my other fosters tolerated each other, they never really played or snuggled together. She put on some weight, but her coat was still rough. The missing eye made her face appear unbalanced, and the fact that she was all black—except for her four white feet—put her at an added disadvantage. That was because, unfortunately, black cats are often the last to get homes.

When I took Marlee to adoption events, she was frightened and sat hunched in the back of her crate. It was the children who were usually the first to exclaim, "Look! This cat only has one eye!" But no one wanted to adopt her.

Lots of things changed when Elsa came along. Like Marlee, Elsa was a stray kitten who had been taken in by our rescue group. She was a beautiful light gray tabby with fur that was smooth and soft. She loved to sit in my lap and purr.

Soon Elsa was playing with the other kitties, including Marlee. But the strange thing I noticed about Elsa was that she kept bumping into furniture and door casings. I began to suspect that she had some type of vision problem.

A trip to the veterinary opthamologist confirmed my fears. Elsa was totally blind! Given that knowledge, I was actually amazed at how well she had learned to navigate most of the obstacles in my house.

Another thing I noticed was that a close bond had begun to form between one-eyed Marlee and blind Elsa. Marlee seemed to sense intuitively that Elsa needed her help, and she offered it freely, serving as a type of seeing-eye cat for her little friend.

Now our rescue group faced a new difficulty. Elsa and Marlee were so reliant on each other that it would be a crime to adopt them out separately. But finding a home for two normal cats together is challenging enough. Finding an adopter who would be willing to take two "special needs" kitties seemed like the impossible dream!

In addition to posting the story of Elsa and Marlee online, I took the two kitties to most of our weekly adoption events.

There was always the chance that someone would see them there, fall in love, and decide to give them a forever-home. And after several weeks, that is exactly what happened.

We were about to fold up shop one Saturday afternoon when a mom and dad came by with their twin daughters, who appeared to be about 11 or 12. The mom told me the family had been thinking about adopting a cat. They hoped they could get a kitten or a young adult who would be with them for many years.

By this time, the girls had discovered Marlee and Elsa. "Mom, this cat is blind!" said one of the twins, reading the kitty's bio. "And this one lost an eye," added the other twin.

I explained that the two cats were quite bonded, and that Marlee helped Elsa get around. "We'd like for them to go to a home where they can stay together," I concluded, "but it's a big responsibility to take on two kitties with special needs."

The twins looked at the cats again and then at their parents. "Oh! Can we adopt them both?" they asked. "Please Mom! Please Dad!" The parents seemed willing to consider the idea, at least, so I sent the family into the store office, where they could get to know Elsa and Marlee a little better. When they came back out, they said they wanted to adopt both cats.

While the mom filled out the application, the girls began taking photos and texting them to their friends. Their dad came over to me. "Kids nowadays," he said with a sigh. "All they want to do is text and play video games and post messages on the internet."

I nodded in agreement.

"We've tried taking away their phones," he went on, "but that just made everybody angry and grumpy. That's why we wanted to get the girls a pet. We thought maybe it would help them see that there are other things in life to care about besides electronic gadgets."

As the family left the store with Marlee and Elsa, I said a prayer that my two "fur-babies" would be happy and well cared for, and that the parents' wish for their daughters would come true.

Over the next few weeks, I called at regular intervals to find out how Marlee and Elsa were doing. I was told that they had gradually learned their way around the house and were now acting as if they had always lived there. The twins played with them often, and the kitties slept in the girls' room at night.

Then one Saturday, while I was again helping with an adoption event, the mom and dad dropped by to say hello. "Where are your daughters?" I asked.

"They volunteer most Saturdays now," said the dad.

"That's wonderful!" I exclaimed. "What sort of volunteer work are they doing?"

"Their school group has been going on outings with kids from the school for the blind," the dad said. "And the blind kids have shown them how they use canes and listen to traffic before crossing the street. They have really helped the sighted kids see things from a whole new perspective, so to speak," he added with a smile.

"Both of our daughters have started learning to read Braille," added the mom. "And sometimes they go hours at a time without sending a single text!"

"It's a minor miracle," added the dad. "And I'm convinced it all started when we adopted Elsa and Marlee. Our daughters saw how devoted those two kitties were to helping each other, and they decided they wanted to do the same thing for somebody."

After the couple left, I just stood there for a while enjoying a warm, tingly feeling of gratitude. Prayers really could be answered, and two kittens who could barely see had been able to open up a whole new world vision for two young girls.

WHO RESCUED WHOM?

*There are hundreds of good reasons
for having a cat, but all you need is one.*

Susy Clemens

I hadn't planned to retire yet, but then the company where I spent more than thirty years of my working life was forced to downsize. They gave me a good severance package, and I was old enough for Social Security, so at least there were no financial worries. I just didn't know what to do with myself. I had never married, so I had no children or grandchildren. I didn't really have any hobbies. The job had been the center of my life, and now it was gone.

"Why don't you travel?" asked my friend Kathy. "I think that's what I would do."

But I didn't see myself as the traveling type. "There's no place I'm very interested in going," I admitted. "And the idea of getting stuck in a bunch of airports because of canceled flights doesn't really thrill me."

"Okay," she said. "Well, maybe you could do some volunteer work."

"Volunteer work?" I said cautiously. "What kind of volunteer work?"

"Well, there are all kinds of organizations that need help. You can take your pick, depending on what you are interested in. You could work at a food bank or a thrift store. You could teach people to read, or you could shelve books in a library. And if you like art," she went on, "you can volunteer at the museum."

"That's a lot of choices," I admitted.

"Another idea," she added, "would be for you to volunteer at the animal shelter, where I work. I didn't mention that one earlier because I didn't know if you liked animals."

"Well, I haven't had any pets since I was a kid. I liked them then, so I guess I still do," I told her. "But isn't it depressing to go there and see all those dogs and cats that nobody wants? And don't they get put to sleep, if the shelter runs out of space?"

"No, this shelter takes every measure to care for animals until they can be placed with a loving family."

I still wasn't convinced that volunteering at a shelter was what I wanted to do. I guess Kathy saw this because she added, "There are lots of ways you can volunteer at the shelter. You don't even have to work with the animals directly. You can do filing or stuff envelopes or help plan fund-raising events."

So I reluctantly agreed to give it a try. I figured it had to be better than sitting around at home, feeling miserable about having lost my job.

The first few times I went, I limited myself to filing. But then I decided to spend some time in the cat room. As soon as I walked in there, the friendliest of the kitties came up and started rubbing against my legs. When I sat down, they jumped in my lap. I petted them, I brushed them, I played with them. I went home covered with cat hair, but feeling calmer and happier than I had felt when I arrived.

Then one day, Kathy told me about a kitten someone had brought in a few days earlier. "We think this little girl was attacked by a coyote. She has a bite wound and a fractured back leg, but she should heal up fine in a few weeks. In the meantime, she needs a nice, quiet home where she can get some cage rest – someplace with no dogs or young children."

"Are you wanting me to– " I began.

"Yes, I thought you might make the perfect foster mom for this little girl," she said with a grin. "Of course, if you don't want to foster her, that's fine. We'll find someone else."

And before I could respond, she asked, "Want to meet her?"

Kathy took me to a back room, lifted a young kitten out of a cage, and put her in my arms. The kitten immediately began to purr loudly. I stroked her, surprised by the softness of her brown-and-black "tortoiseshell" colored fur.

"What happened to her tail?" I asked in surprise. "It's like half of it is missing!"

"We think it got bitten off by the coyote. We've named her 'Bobbi,' because she has a bobbed tail."

I laughed. Bobbi continued purring and looking up at me with wide green eyes.

Of course, I took her home and fostered her until her injuries healed up. By the time she was ready for adoption, she had completely won my heart, and I adopted her myself. I still marvel at how much love, joy, and purpose my little kitty brings me every day.

"I really have to thank you for your suggestion that I volunteer," I said to Kathy one day. "You can't believe what a difference it has made in my life."

"I can believe it," Kathy said with a wink. "Why do you think I suggested it?"

SOME IMPORTANT THINGS
I'VE LEARNED FROM MY CAT

Enjoy the present moment.
It won't last long, and it will never come again.

Slow down, relax, take a nap now and then.
It's a good way to refresh the mind and reenergize the body.

Take time to play. It will keep you feeling young.

Any time you have requests or opinions,
state them politely, but firmly.

If you aren't heard the first time, repeat yourself until you are!

Make one chair your special favorite and revisit it often.

Show your affection openly. There's nothing like a little purring
and closeness to alleviate stress.

When it comes to food,
always show yourself to be a true connoisseur.

Try to spend some time each day keeping yourself clean and
neatly groomed.

Never lose your sense of curiosity.
There is a whole world out there, just waiting to be explored.

LITTLE THINGS MATTER, TOO

Nothing is too small a subject for prayer, because nothing is too small to be the subject od God's care.

I was always very careful to keep my cat Max indoors. But the day the repairman was here, going in and out, Max saw his opportunity. He rushed through the front door and into our busy street where, to my horror, he was hit by a car.

"I'm afraid his back has been broken," my veterinarian told me. I could tell she was trying to be as gentle as she could. "Max will never be able to use his back legs again."

The tears that I had been trying to keep under control burst out again. "But he's only ten months old!" I wailed. "This is so unfair!"

"I know," Dr. Stewart told me. She put an arm around my shoulders. "So many things happen in life that are out of our control."

"What do we do now?" I asked her. "Will Max have to be put to sleep?"

"That would be one option," she said quietly. "He will probably be able to drag himself around with his front legs, but that isn't a great way for a cat to live his life." She paused, then added, "another possibility would be to get him a wheelchair."

"A wheelchair?" I said in surprise. "They make wheelchairs for cats?" "Yes, they originally just made them for dogs, and now they make them for cats, too. The good ones are a little pricey, but at least you would still have a cat who's alive and able to get around. We need to keep Max here at the clinic for a couple more days until he's stable," she went on. "You can think about your options in the meantime."

When I brought my sweet gray kitty home, and looked into his bright green eyes, I saw a lot of trust and determination there. This was not a cat who was ready to give up on life. And I wasn't ready to give up on him either. I decided I would get him a wheelchair.

The problem was that I had already maxed out my credit card on vet bills. How could I possibly afford a wheelchair for Max?

I spent several sleepless nights worrying and running budget numbers over and over in my head. Then I went to my group. I felt a little silly, asking them to pray about a wheelchair for a cat. After all, there were people with much more serious issues who needed prayer.

But the members of the group not only prayed, they also offered practical suggestions. One man offered to set up one of those sites on the internet where you ask people to make donations to your cause. We set a target amount, and I provided several photos of Max, including a video of him pulling himself around by his front legs.

A couple of the women in the group suggested we have a yard sale to raise some additional money. I was humbled that all of these people cared so much about me and about Max.

Of course, we also continued to pray, and I believe that God heard our prayers. We came very close to meeting the target donation goal we had set on the internet, and the yard sale proceeds put us over the top. I ended up with enough to buy Max a custom-fitted wheelchair, plus pay off most of his medical bills.

I was so afraid that, after all our efforts, Max would refuse to use the wheelchair. But I introduced him to it gradually, and before long, he was happily trundling around the house. I even started taking him to hospitals and nursing homes, where he was very popular and a big inspiration to many of the patients.

Looking back, I was so very grateful that I decided not to have Max euthanized after his accident. He was a cat with a strong will to live, and I had honored that and learned from it. I was also reminded that God really does answer prayers, and He answers them in abundance – even prayers for a cat!

LOVE TO THE RESCUE

We are born of love; love is our mother.
Rumi

I've seen a lot of amazing things during my many years as a firefighter, but one thing I will always remember is seeing a mother cat carry her kittens, one by one, out of a burning house.

We had been called out mid-morning to fight a fire in an abandoned house. A neighbor noticed the smoke and called 911, but by that time, the blaze had a real head start on us.

My job was to drive one of the rigs, so I was standing a little back from the actual firefighting operations, monitoring communications, when a boy came running up to me. He looked to be 11 or 12 years old.

"Son, you need to keep farther away from the fire," I told him. "It's not safe here."

"But mister, you've got to come save a cat!" he exclaimed.

"What cat?"

"It's a mama cat, and she's busy carrying her kittens out of the fire, trying to save them."

"Show me where she is," I told him, and he led me around to the back of the house.

Sure enough, as we watched, a little cat came out from under the back porch with a kitten in her mouth. She carried it into the bushes some twenty yards away, left it there, and then hurried back toward the house.

"Does the cat belong to anyone around here?" I asked the boy.

"No," he said, "she's a stray. My mom feeds her sometimes, and so do the other neighbors."

Just then, the cat reemerged from the house with another kitten.

"Stay here," I told the boy. "I'm going to try to get hold of her." I moved to the spot where the kittens were being deposited. There were three there already, crying loudly, and as the mother cat added the fourth one, I tried to grab her. She hissed and bit at my gloves, then turned and ran back to the fiery house again.

The boy had not heeded my request to stay put, and now he was at my elbow, asking "Is she going to get burned up?"

"I certainly hope not," I told him. I didn't mention that the cat's fur was already singed and sooty in places.

Just then a woman came rushing up. "There you are, Lucas!" she exclaimed. "You need to leave this nice man alone so he can do his job and fight the fire. Now, come on home with me."

"But Mom, I'm helping save Sweetie's kittens!" Lucas said. "And here she comes with another one!" He pointed first to the bundle of kittens at our feet and then at the approaching mama cat.

By now the cat was moving more slowly and painfully. She seemed somewhat disoriented, but eventually made her way to us. Dropping the last kitten, she sniffed them all and then lay down beside them, clearly exhausted.

The woman crouched down and began to stroke her. "Oh, poor Sweetie!" she said. "I didn't even know you had kittens. No wonder you've been so hungry lately!"

"I think I'd better give her some oxygen," I said. "But I need to take her around front, where our equipment is. Do you have a box or something to put the kittens in?"

"Yes, we'll find you something, don't worry," She turned to Lucas. "Run and get one of those boxes out of the basement," she told him, "as fast as you can, Lucas."

"Thank you," I said. Then I picked up the mother cat and hurried around to the front of the burning house. I hooked up an oxygen mask and held it over the cat's face. She was a tortoiseshell, and from what I could tell, her markings were quite lovely. A couple of her kittens had been torties, too, another was an orange tabby, and the other two had appeared to be mostly black.

I had learned a lot about cats and dogs and every other kind of animal from my sister, Susan. We had had every kind of pet imaginable while we were growing up, and no one in the family was surprised when Susan decided to become a veterinarian. For the past few years, she had headed up the clinic at the local animal shelter.

I dialed the clinic's number now, while still holding the oxygen mask with my other hand. The receptionist was able to put me through to Susan, once I explained who I was and that I had an emergency on my hands.

"I'm giving the cat oxygen now," I told my sister. "It looks like she's got some serious burns on her feet and ears. Maybe some other places, too."

"How about the kittens? Did they get any smoke inhalation? Any burns?"

"I haven't really had a chance to look at them," I admitted. "Some people are bringing a box to put them in."

"We really need to get them over here to the clinic as soon as possible," Susan said. "Where are you? Where is the fire?"

I gave her the address.

"Okay, I'll get somebody to go right over there and pick them up," Susan said. "If you get a chance, give those kittens some oxygen, too. That was one brave kitty, saving her babies like that!"

The next few days were crucial in the recovery of Sweetie and her five kittens, but they all pulled through. Sweetie lost her eyelashes and part of her left ear, which gave her a charmingly off-kilter look. One of the kittens ended up with a slightly shorter tail, due to some burns on the tip of it. But in general, the whole feline family came out of the experience in good shape, thanks to Sweetie's actions.

Susan called the TV news station to find out if they were interested in the story, which they were. They wanted to interview me, along with Susan. I suggested they include Lucas, as well. The boy and his mother had visited Sweetie and the kittens several times at the shelter.

Lucas was delighted to appear on camera. I thought he would mostly talk about his own role in the rescue, but instead he talked about Sweetie and how brave she was.

"She's a mother, and she had kittens. She loved her babies, and that's why she risked her life to save them," he told the reporter. "It's what mothers do."

I felt tears sting my eyes, and I saw some other people also blinking and wiping their eyes.

The animal shelter received over one hundred applications to adopt Sweetie and her kittens. Excellent homes were soon chosen, and several other good applicants ended up adopting other cats and kittens from the shelter. So there were many happy endings.

Every time Susan and I talked about Sweetie and her little family after that, we pondered the meaning of her actions. Had it been pure instinct, or could cats be said to exhibit love? In the end, we had to admit that Lucas was probably right when he claimed that Sweetie saved her kittens because she loved them. "It's what mothers do," he had said. What a beautiful thought.

IVE LEARNED...

Who would believe such pleasure
from a wee ball o' fur?
Proverb

I've learned that when you sniff my face,
your whiskers tickle me, and I laugh.

I've learned that when you walk across my keyboard,
very strange words appear on the screen.

I've learned that if I'm making chicken salad,
it's almost impossible to keep you away.

I've learned that if you are purring beside me in bed,
it's much easier to fall asleep.

I've learned that you give me the kind of love
I can only call unconditional.

I've learned that you make my life complete,
in so many wonderful ways!

BELIEVING IN MIRACLES

Dogs remember faces, cats places.

Proverb

Our big brown-and-black Maine Coon cat, Louie, went missing on the same day our neighbors moved to a town 200 miles away. Of course, we didn't realize right away that Louie was missing, but when he didn't show up for supper or for breakfast the next day, we started getting worried.

We didn't know how old Louie was when we first adopted him, but we had had him for about five years. He was the only pet our six-year-old son Pete had ever known, and Pete adored him.

"Maybe he wandered off and got lost somehow," I suggested. "Or else he might have wondered into somebody's garage and been shut in."

"Or maybe the Smiths took him with them when they moved," Pete said.

"Why would the Smiths take our cat?" asked my husband Tim. "They know how much we love Louie."

"Yes," persisted Pete, "but maybe Louie got inside the moving truck, just to check things out, and the movers didn't know he was in there, and they closed the door and drove off."

Tim and I looked at each other, and I had a sinking feeling, knowing Pete's scenario could actually have taken place.

"Well," I said, "let's hope that's not what happened, because if it did, Charlie is a long ways from home by now."

"Could you call the Smiths and ask if they've seen Louie?" Pete asked.

"Sure," Tim said. "I'll call them right now."

Mr. and Mrs. Smith had not seen Louie. They reported that the moving van had been quickly unloaded while they were mostly inside the house, supervising the placement of furniture and boxes. But when they checked with their teenaged daughter, she said she had noticed a cat hanging around for a while after the movers left. At the time, she thought it looked sort of like Louie, but then decided it couldn't possibly be him. The cat had disappeared shortly after that.

The Smiths promised to put up flyers in their new neighborhood, if we emailed one to them. So I got busy creating a flyer and sent it to them.

We decided to proceed as if we believed Louie was still somewhere in our own neighborhood, too. Tim and Pete went out searching, calling Louie's name, and asking people if they had seen our cat. We looked for him for many days and literally papered every light pole in the area with Louie's picture and our contact information. We made regular calls to the registry for lost pets, and to all the local shelters and veterinary clinics.

We rented a humane trap from the animal control department and put it out faithfully every night for over two weeks. We caught one of the neighbors' cats and two opossums, or maybe it was the same opossum twice. But no Louie.

After about a month, we finally had to admit that Louie was really gone. At least, Tim and I admitted it, but Pete would not. "He'll come back," the boy insisted. "I think he moved far away to where the Smiths went, but he's going to come back here because he loves us best."

Tim and I could only sigh and give our son a hug.

When Louie had been gone for about three months, we tried to talk Pete into adopting another cat. "How about a cute little kitten?" Tim suggested. "Or even two cute little kittens?"

But Pete shook his head. "We can't get another cat," he explained patiently, "because if we have another cat here, then when Louie gets back, he'll think we don't love him anymore."

"It's okay," I told Tim. "We just have to wait until he's ready."

Autumn arrived, bringing all those orange and yellow leaves that Louie used to love playing in. Then it was winter, and the snow came. On Christmas Eve, after a nice little family dinner, we were sitting in the living room, talking about the idea of miracles...especially the miracle of a baby born in the manger.

Suddenly, there was a lull in the conversation, and we all heard it: a loud meowing at the back door!

"It's Louie!" cried Pete, as he scrambled to his feet and ran to open the door.

I followed him, already opening my mouth to tell him the cat couldn't possibly be Louie. But it was! A matted, bedraggled, scrawny cat walked in the door, and he was clearly Louie. Pete threw himself on the cat and began hugging him. Louie responded by purring and giving out those "I'm hungry!" meows I remembered so well.

We never knew for sure where Louie had been during those six months he was missing, but we strongly suspected that Pete had been right when he guessed that Louie got transported by mistake in the moving van.

Our veterinarian agreed that it appeared Louie had been on a long journey of some type. His paws were sore, and he had lost several pounds. His fur was so matted and full of burrs that it had to be shaved down and allowed to grow out again.

"I don't know how they do it," the vet said, "but some cats seem to have an instinct that allows them to find their way home over long distances. There are other cases of this sort of thing happening."

Pete proclaimed Louie's return the best Christmas present he had ever gotten. In fact, Pete told us that he had been praying to the Baby Jesus throughout Advent for just this miracle to occur.

I was more than a little impressed by our son's prayers and his unwavering faith in the power of love to bring his cat back to him. For it must have been love. What else would have guided a cat over such a long distance to be back with the people who cared the most about him?

LESSONS IN INDEPENDENCE

Cats are a mysterious kind of folk.
There is more passing in their minds than we are aware of.
Sir Walter Scott

The cat is domestic only as far as suits its own ends.
Saki (Hector Hugh Munro)

I am the Cat who walks by himself,
and all places are alike to me."
Rudyard Kipling

Cat: a pygmy lion who loves mice, hates dogs,
and patronizes human beings."
Oliver Herford

In a cat's eye, all things belong to cats.
Proverb

A SPECIAL GIFT

Once [a cat] has given its love,
what absolute confidence, what fidelity of affection!

Théophile Gautier

My husband Bill was not crazy about the idea of our adopting a kitten for our daughter Emily. But she kept working at convincing him, and eventually she wore him down. Emily was eight and had recently been diagnosed with Type I diabetes. I think Bill would have done almost anything for Emily at that point, and I felt the same way.

We soon got into a routine with Emily's diabetes treatment – testing her blood sugar and administering prescribed doses of insulin. Still, we worried about her and about what might happen if she ever suffered from hypoglycemia (low blood sugar) and didn't realize what was going on.

But then we got the kitten, and he was a nice distraction from thinking about diabetes. He was a gray tabby with white markings on his feet, face, and chest. Emily named him Button. "Because he's cute as a button," she explained.

It didn't take long before Button was settled in at our house and starting to get into all types of mischief. At five months, he was already big enough that he could jump onto the kitchen counter, so we had to remember to keep all the food put away.

Button also learned how to get into the trash, so we had to buy a much heavier waste can with a lid. He also loved to pull the towels off the racks in the bathroom, climb the shower curtain, and shred the toilet paper.

At mealtimes, the kitten repeatedly jumped into our laps and from there onto the table. Emily thought this was a cute trick, but Bill and I were not amused. We instituted a No Cats on the Table rule, but it was hard to enforce. We tried to follow the advice on a website, suggesting that squirting a cat with a little water from a spray bottle might get the message across. Emily really disliked that training tactic.

Bill started getting grumpy about having Button in the house. He complained about the kitten's mischievous behavior, about the smell of the litter box, the sharpness of Button's claws, and about the cost of cat food.

"Maybe we should just take him back to the rescue group," he suggested to me one night after Emily had gone to bed.

"Don't even think about it," I warned. "You know how our daughter adores that cat!"

"Yes," he admitted, "but she'll get over it. We can promise her a trip to a theme park or something."

"That's not the same, and you know it," I told him. "Button is just acting like a kitten, and in a few months, he'll calm down."

"Well, I certainly hope so," Bill said. He had apparently given up for now, but I was pretty sure the topic would come up again.

Everything changed a couple of nights later. We had gone to bed as usual and were sound asleep. I woke up to find Button scratching at my arm rather frantically, then nipping my nose. Annoyed, I lifted the kitten off me and dropped him on the floor. But he instantly jumped back on the bed and started pawing at me again. I wondered what he was even doing in our room. He always spent the night with Emily.

I sat up in bed, and that's when I heard Emily calling. Jumping out of bed, I hurried down the hall to her room.

"Mommy, I don't feel good," she said.

"Is your blood sugar low?" I asked anxiously.

"I don't know. I just felt funny. Button woke me up. I tried to get out of bed, but I got too dizzy."

"Okay," I said, trying to keep my voice calm. "Stay right there. I'll get the glucose tablets."

I ran into Bill in the hall. "What's going on?" he said.

"It's Emily," I told him. "Low blood sugar."

"I'll go downstairs and get what we need," Bill said quickly.

I went back to Emily's room to sit with her.

"How do you feel?" I asked her.

"I'm really weak and shaky," she told me, "and I have a headache."

"Daddy went to get the glucose," I told her. "You'll feel better in no time."

"Mommy, what's happening?" Emily asked.

"Honey, your blood sugar was dropping" I said, as I bent down to give her a kiss. "We'll get you feeling better."

Bill returned with the glucose tablets and blood testing kit. As we sat with Emily, waiting for the tablets to take effect, Bill said, "It's a good thing you woke up when you did."

"Button woke me up," Emily told him.

"He did?" Bill said in surprise.

"Yeah. I sat up in bed, but I was really dizzy, so I had to lie down again. I called, but nobody heard me."

"I guess that's when Button came and woke me up," I said.

"He woke you up, too?" Bill asked. "Well, that was one busy little cat!"

"Uh-huh," Emily said, stroking the kitten, who was sitting on her chest. "He's my hero."

"What he did was pretty amazing," Bill admitted. "I've heard of dogs being trained to alert people to hypoglycemia, but I never thought a cat could do it."

"Well, we certainly know that Button is a clever kitty," I said. "And I guess he proved it again tonight."

"I think Button proved he has a reason for being here with us. He knows how to take care of me."

It was Bill who answered in a voice that was soft but certain. "I'm sure you are right Emily. Button proved he has a purpose right here in this home, at this time, and in these circumstances. He definitely is our special gift."

RULES FOR THE CAT

1. The cat may sleep on the bed, but only on the foot of the bed.
2. Okay, the cat is allowed to sleep up against the human, but not on the pillow.
3. The cat can sleep on the pillow, but definitely not on the human's face.
4. Fine! The human will adjust his or her sleeping position to accommodate the comfort of the cat.
5. The cat is allowed on the furniture, but not during shedding season.
6. Okay, the cat can shed on the furniture, but no claws will be sharpened there.
7. Very well, the human will invest in expensive scratching posts and plan on replacing the furniture periodically.
8. The cat may jump on the kitchen counter, but not while food is being prepared.
9. All right, the cat can be on the counter during food preparation, but must maintain a respectful distance at all times.
10. "Respectful distance" means further than one inch!
11. The cat is definitely not allowed on the dining room table.
12. Well, okay, but not during meals.
13. No! No! The cat will not eat off the human's plate!

RULES FOR THE HUMAN

1. The human needs to learn that making rules for a cat is impossible!

JUST FOR THE ASKING

*A prayer is the shortest distance between
your question and God's answer.*

My granddaughter Ashley called me one evening to tell
me that she and her husband were going on vacation to
Europe. They would be away for about three weeks.

"I'm so excited!" she said. "I can hardly wait!"

"I'd be excited, too," I told her. "I'm sure you will have a
good time."

"Yes," Ashley agreed, "but I'm worried about leaving Lily.
Could you possibly keep her for us while we're gone?"

"Of course I can," I assured her. "I'd love having Lily
here."

Lily was the little white cat Ashley had adopted two
months before. She was so shy that I had never actually seen
her. But Ashley often sent me pictures. Apparently, Lily was
quite a nice kitty once you got to know her.

The night before the trip, Ashley brought Lily over, along
with her litter box and food. I peered into the carrier and
could just barely make out a cat cowering in the back of it.

"She might hide from you at first," Ashley said, "but after she gets over being nervous, you'll see what a wonderful cat she is."

"Well, I hope it doesn't take her long to get used to me," I said. "You and Jack have a fun trip, and don't worry about a thing. I'll take good care of Lily."

"Thanks, Grandma," said Ashley, giving me a hug before she hurried off.

I opened the door to Lily's carrier and looked in again. She stared back with wide green eyes and shrank into an even smaller ball of fur.

"Okay," I told her. "I will just leave the door open, and you can come out whenever you want to and make yourself at home."

I set up the litter box and put some food in Lily's dish in the kitchen. When I went to bed, two hours later, the cat was still huddled in the back end of her carrier.

But the next morning, she was gone. That is, she was gone from the carrier. Her food was uneaten, and the litter was untouched. I launched a search, but I couldn't find her anywhere. Having some arthritis in my knees and back made it hard for me to look under and behind furniture, but I did my best.

I finally gave up the search, reasoning that when Lily got hungry enough, she would appear. I went out several times to run errands, and I worried each time I opened the door that Lily would go streaking out. I watched closely for any escaping white kitty, and even though I didn't see one, I couldn't help having the nagging doubt that I had somehow missed seeing her.

By that evening, I was becoming seriously concerned. Lily still hadn't come out to eat or use the litter box. How long could a cat go without doing these things?

Then Ashley called from Germany to ask how Lily was doing. I didn't want to lie, so I said, "Well, so far she's kept a low profile and I haven't seen much of her."

Ashley laughed. "That sounds like Lily, all right. Is she eating much?"

"No, not much," I admitted.

"She will," Ashley said. "It just takes her a while to get over being scared." She went on to say that she and Jack were having a wonderful time, and that she was so glad she didn't have to worry about Lily.

Before I went to bed, I searched again, but still couldn't find my granddaughter's cat. How could I have lost an entire cat in a small, one-bedroom apartment? And how would I ever be able to tell Ashley that her beloved cat was gone?

Lying wide awake in the dark that night, it finally occurred to me that there was Someone I could ask for help. So I began praying. "Lord," I said, "Lily is one of the beautiful little creatures that You have made, so I know You can speak to her and she will understand. Just tell her that I want to be her friend, and she doesn't need to be afraid of me. Please, God," I finished, "Ashley entrusted me with this task, and I don't want to let her down."

After I prayed, I felt much more peaceful, and I went right to sleep. When I got up the next morning, I saw that the food in Lily's dish was gone, and she had used the litter box. The cat herself was still nowhere to be seen, but at least I knew she was somewhere in the apartment.

"Thank You, God!" I said in relief.

Later in the day, while I was having lunch with a friend, Lily apparently came out and ate more food. I made a point of keeping the food dish and water bowl full. I also scooped the litter box any time I saw that it had been used. But I still hadn't seen Lily, and I didn't know where she was hiding.

A couple of nights later, after reading and falling into a deep sleep, I was suddenly awakened by a tickling sensation on my face. I thought it was a bug, but when I reached up to brush it away, my hand met soft fur.

"Lily!" I whispered softly. I was afraid to try to pet her

because I didn't want to frighten her. She sniffed at me for a short time and then settled down on the foot of the bed and began to groom herself.

That was the beginning of a very special friendship. By the time Ashley and Jack got home, Lily was regularly sitting in my lap while I knitted and watched TV. She loved trying to play with the yarn and knitting needles. At night, she snuggled up next to me in bed.

We never figured out for sure where Lily had been hiding, but when Jack crawled around and checked out all the possibilities, he found an opening that would have allowed her to crawl up into the frame of my box springs. Anyway, the important thing was that she eventually came out and let me enjoy her company.

I mostly reflected upon all that time to think that I had spent fretting and worrying before I turned the matter over to God. All I had to do was reach out. Help was there, just for the asking.

KITTENS BLESS US
WITH LAUGHTER

There is no more intrepid explorer than a kitten.

Jules Champfleury

A kitten is the most
irresistible comedian in the world.
Its wide-open eyes gleam
with wonder and mirth.
It darts madly at nothing at all,
and then, as though suddenly
checked in the pursuit,
prances sideways on its hind legs
with ridiculous agility and zeal.

Agnes Repplier

Kittens believe that all nature
is occupied with their diversion.

F.A. Paradis de Moncrif

A kitten is so flexible
that she is almost double;
the hind parts are equivalent
to another kitten
with which the forepart plays.
She does not discover
that her tail belongs to her
until you tread on it.

Henry David Thoreau

It is a very inconvenient habit of kittens . . .
that whatever you say to them,
they always purr.

Lewis Carroll

AMPLY REWARDED

To know that even one life has breathed easier because you have lived. This is to have succeeded.

Ralph Waldo Emerson

When I was a senior in high school, I got a job at a fast-food restaurant. My parents had agreed to buy me a car, if I paid for the insurance, which was expensive because of my being a male teenager. So some of my part-time salary went for premiums, and I could spend the rest however I liked.

At the restaurant where I worked, an old gray cat used to come around often, and everybody called him Tom. Our manager, Ken, was a big animal lover, so he didn't mind if we gave Tom some of the chicken and fish leftovers. Several neighbors knew Tom, too, and brought food over for him.

Ken's wife, Sally, was probably Tom's biggest fan. She had tried more than once to get hold of him so that her rescue group could find a proper home for him. But Tom wasn't having any of that. He would arrive at least once a day to eat, and he would let people get fairly close to him, but he didn't let anybody touch him. Sally had even tried using a humane trap to capture Tom, but he was much too smart to get caught in one of those things.

Then one day, Tom stopped coming. He had missed a day now and then in the past, but it wasn't like him to be gone for several days in a row. Sally checked with Animal Control, but they hadn't found a cat matching Tom's description.

None of us knew what to think, but we began to fear the worst. Ken told us to stop leaving food out for Tom because he didn't want to attract rats.

"Just keep an eye out for him," Ken said. "If he shows up again, we'll feed him."

Ten days had passed when Tom finally came back. I'm the one who saw him first. It was the night shift, and I was on break, out behind the restaurant, texting with my girlfriend. Looking up, I could just make out a bedraggled-looking Tom limping slowly across the parking lot.

"Gotta go. Cat's back!" I texted quickly and pocketed my cell phone. I stuck my head in the kitchen door and called to Ken.

"I think he's hurt," I told my boss when he came out the door.

"Looks like he's in pretty bad shape," Ken agreed. "I wonder what happened to him. Are you on break?" he asked.

"Yeah, I've got about five minutes left."

"Okay, stay here and watch Tom. I'm going to get some food and water and call Sally." He disappeared inside.

The cat was still making his slow, painful way toward me. I crouched down and started talking to him. I could see that he was dragging his left front leg without putting any weight on it. I was amazed at how close he came before he sat down, seemingly exhausted. In the glow of the building's floodlight, I could see that Tom had a bad wound or two. He looked thin, and his fur was dirty and matted.

Ken came back, carrying a crumbled fish patty and a dish of water. He put these down near Tom and then backed up. "Sally's on her way," he told me in a low voice. "She said if there is any way we can get hold of Tom, she will take him to the emergency clinic."

One of the other employees showed up at the back door, carrying several dish towels. "That poor kitty!" she said as she handed the towels to Ken. "He looks like he's been through the wars!"

"Is that how you're going to capture him," I asked, "with dish towels?"

"Maybe," Ken said. "We'll see if Sally has a better idea."

Tom, meanwhile, had crept forward and begun to lap water from the dish. Finally, he turned his attention to the fish. He sniffed it, nibbled a bit, and then sat, looking at us.

"Guess he's not very hungry," Ken said.

"He probably doesn't feel good," the girl in the doorway said.

"Probably not," Ken agreed.

"I've got to get back to work," I said reluctantly, then headed inside.

Sally arrived shortly after that. I didn't know she was there until she came into the kitchen. "I've got him!" she told us. "I put him in a carrier and he's in my car right now. I'm taking him to the clinic."

"How did you manage to pick him up?" I asked.

"It was actually easy," she said. "I just wrapped him in the towels. He didn't even try to struggle or bite. I guess he was finally ready to let somebody help him." She turned toward the door. "I'll update you all as soon as I can," she said as she left.

We were closing up, about an hour later, when Ken got a call from Sally. "It's worse than we thought," he reported.

"Tom's wounds are badly infected, he's running a high fever, and his leg is broken in a couple of places. The vet wasn't sure Tom would even make it through the night. He suggested that Sally go ahead and have Tom put to sleep."

"What did Sally say to that?" I asked, although I was pretty sure I knew the answer. "She said no, of course," Ken replied with a smile. "She thinks Tom has the will to live, and Sally is usually right about these things."

When I went to bed that night, I had trouble falling asleep. All I could think about was Tom and how pitiful he had looked. I didn't realize how fond I had become of the big, aloof kitty, and how much I was hoping he would pull through, even though I knew the odds were stacked against him.

The next evening, when I was at work, Sally stopped by to tell us that Tom was improving. He was on antibiotics and IV fluids, so his temperature was back to normal, and the infection would clear up in a week or so. The bad news was that an orthopedist had looked at the x-rays of Tom's leg and said that surgery would be needed to correct the problem.

"Unfortunately, the surgery is going to cost a couple thousand dollars," Sally said, "and I don't know where we're going to get that kind of money. Our rescue group certainly doesn't have it."

"We'll figure out a way to raise the money," I said quickly. "We all care about Tom, and we want to help him."

Sally sighed. "I hope we can do it. Did I tell you how old the vet thinks Tom is?"

I shook my head.

"He said he's probably around twelve, or maybe even older."

"No way!" I said.

"Well, when you get a really close look at him, you can see that he's been through a lot," Sally said. "His teeth are bad, too, so he'll probably lose a bunch of them."

"Poor Tom."

"I just hope we can get him fixed up and find him a home where he can live out the rest of his life in comfort."

"We will. Don't worry," I said, trying to sound more confident than I felt.

Soon our small staff room became the site of some serious planning to raise money for Tom's medical expenses. Because Ken was sympathetic to the cause, we were allowed to put donation boxes next to the cash registers. We printed out flyers with Tom's picture and a link to an online fund-raising site we had set up.

Meanwhile, Sally's rescue group swung into high gear to get contributions for Tom. Ken gave the okay to hold a car wash in the restaurant parking lot. It was so successful that we did a second one. We also held a big yard sale.

Finally, Sally reported that we had raised enough funds to cover all Tom's medical expenses. By then, he was already recovering from his surgery. At first, he had to have complete cage rest, so Sally kept him at a facility run by her rescue group. As Tom got used to being handled by humans, he became quite affectionate. When I went to visit him, he sat in my lap purring loudly. Every time I stopped petting him, he began head-butting me, demanding more attention.

Tom had turned out to be the perfect cat in many ways, except for one thing: he really didn't like other cats. Or dogs.

"We're not sure how Tom got injured," Sally told me, "but the vet thinks he might have been attacked by a coyote. He had several bite wounds, and that's why he had such a bad infection."

"So have you found a home for him?" I asked.

"No, not yet," she said. "It's hard to find someone who will adopt an older cat, and those who are willing to do it usually have other pets."

I could see the problem, but I thought maybe – just maybe – I also saw a solution.

That evening at dinner with my parents, I found myself feeling nervous, but I was determined to make my case. So after swallowing a bite of lasagna and taking a big drink of water, I said, "Remember Tom, that cat we've been trying to save?"

"Yes, of course," my mom said. "How is he doing?"

"He's doing great," I said. "He still has a cast on his leg, but he can already walk around a little bit on it."

"How much money did you end up raising?" my dad asked.

"I'm not sure, exactly, but I think it was like $2500."

"Wow," Dad said, his eyes wide. "That's a lot of money to spend on one cat".

"Yes, but it was worth it," I said quickly. "Tom has turned out to be the sweetest, most wonderful cat ever. Now all we have to do is find him a home."

"Uh-huh," my mother said without much interest.

"So I've been thinking maybe you'd like to go meet him sometime," I said, feeling like the conversation was beginning to flounder.

"And why would we want to meet him?" my dad asked, suspiciously.

"Oh, I know where this is going," Mom broke in. "You're thinking we're going to adopt an old, half-wild cat who is probably going to need a lot of expensive medical care the rest of his life."

"Well, he really needs a home," I said apologetically, "and it has to be a home where there are no cats or dogs already, because he doesn't like them."

"But, Son—" my dad began.

"We used to have a cat, years ago, when I was growing up. Remember? I loved that cat!"

My parents sighed and exchanged glances.

"I don't think this is a good time for us to get a cat," my mom began.

"Just come to the shelter and meet Tom, at least," I pleaded. "Then if you decide not to adopt him, I won't pester you anymore about it."

"You promise?" Dad asked.

"Promise."

So my parents met Tom, and the rest, as people say "was history." It was a case of mutual and instant admiration. Within a week, the big gray kitty had come to live at our house.

One day at work, not long after that, Ken took me aside and said "Sally informed me I should give you a raise, just because of everything you've done for Tom. But I told her that's not quite how it works."

I laughed. "I know," I told him. "I didn't help Tom because I wanted a raise. I helped Tom because I care about Tom."

"That's what I thought," Ken said.

"But I will tell you this," I added. "I've learned that the good feeling you get when you've helped somebody may be every bit as good as getting a pay raise."

"Hmm, so does this mean I don't ever have to give you any raises?" Ken asked.

"Well, no, I didn't say that, exactly."

He laughed. "Get back to work," he said. "You may be due for a raise pretty soon anyway, just to let you know."

I went back to work, feeling warm and happy all over. But I didn't feel that way because of the promise of a raise. I felt that way because of a big gray cat named Tom.

THE MIGHTY HUNTER

We grow great by dreams.
Woodrow Wilson

I am the mighty hunter!
All through the house I slink
In search of dancing laser lights
Or droplets in the sink.

When stalking, I am stealthy,
I wait so patiently.
The twitching of my tail's the only
Moving part of me.

My whiskers start to quiver
As I look all around.
I see a tiny hint of movement,
Then I hear a sound.

I'm filled with great excitement,
A feline hunter's joy.
I pounce! And now I've captured it—
My favorite catnip toy!

CHANGING DIRECTIONS

Go confidently in the direction of your dreams.
Live the life you have imagined.
Henry David Thoreau

I was just leaving work when I got a text from my friend Chelsea. "kittens at risk" it read, "can u adopt 1"?

"What's going on?" I texted back.

"Shelter full" came the reply. Chelsea volunteered at the local animal shelter when she wasn't attending classes at the university. She adored animals of all kinds, and already had more than her legal quota of them. Otherwise, I imagined that she would be taking a new batch of kittens to her own house.

Chelsea was smart to ask me, though, because I had actually been thinking about getting a kitten. Now that I was out of high school and working at the grocery store, I could finally afford a place of my own. It wasn't much of a place – just a little mobile home that I was renting – but I was allowed to have one pet, which was more than my parents let me have when I was living at home.

So I went to the shelter and came home with an adorable black-and-white kitten. She had tuxedo markings, so it always looked like she was getting ready to step up on a podium and start conducting an orchestra. She reminded me of Charlie Chaplin in some of those old silent movies, so I named her Charli.

I was really glad I adopted her. She was talkative and she loved to play. She purred happily anytime I picked her up or petted her. At night, snuggled with me in bed.

I had grown up as the oldest in a family with five kids, and even though I loved my parents and siblings, I had been eager to move into a place of my own, where I could have some peace and privacy. But I had never lived alone before, and I hadn't realized how lonely I might feel sometimes. Charli helped me get over that feeling, and I was thankful to her for that.

Then one cold night in early autumn, I ended up with even more to thank Charli for. I had gone to bed exhausted after a long day on my feet, working the cash register at the grocery store. At some point, in the middle of a dream, I woke up enough to realize that Charli was meowing and pawing at my cheek and nose.

"Quit it, Charli," I muttered and threw an arm over my face.

But then she became even more urgent, nipping at my elbow and forearm.

"Don't!" I said, trying to push her away. But she came right back, pawing at me again and meowing insistently.

I reached out for her and realized she was busily sniffing the air. So I sniffed, too, and that's when I smelled it. Gas! I sat up in bed and even thought I could hear the hiss of escaping gas, maybe from that little closet in the hallway where the hot water heater was.

"We've got to get out of here!" I exclaimed, snatching up Charli and thrusting her into her carrier. I threw on some shoes and a coat, grabbed my purse and phone, and ran out the door.

Later, the gas department told me that if there had been some spark in my little mobile home while that leak was going on, the whole place probably would have exploded. All it would have taken was for the furnace to kick in. They told me it was a good thing I got out when I did.

Of course, I gave Charli most of the credit. I had never been a very religious person, even though I grew up going to Sunday School, but after that night I began to believe that Somebody was really looking out for me. I decided it was that Somebody who had sent Charli to me to save my life.

When I talked to Chelsea about my new feelings, she said, "Well, you may be right about God's sending Charli to you, but I'd like to be honest with you. God wants us to do all we can for ourselves, too. You need to do something with your life, Girl. Are you going to be happy working in the grocery store forever? What would you really like to do, if you had your choice?"

"I'd like to be a nurse," I admitted. "But my parents can't afford to send me to school."

"Okay, then, we'll have to figure out how you can pay for nursing school on your own. There are probably some scholarships, student loans, work-study programs, stuff like that. Go online and see what you can find out."

I nodded, feeling encouraged.

"You should be able to get some of your basic credits at the community college. That wouldn't be too expensive, and you could pay for it with what you're making at your job now."

"And then I could get a scholarship or loan to finish my degree."

"Exactly!" she said, giving me a hug. "You always got good grades when we were in high school. I can't believe you haven't already figured all this out for yourself."

Chelsea was kidding me a little, but I began to think seriously about the path I'd been on. "I guess I was just so focused on being on my own away from home that I didn't think things through. This little kitten saved my life, and that kind of put things in perspective. And you, my best friend, are giving me a nudge to get me thinking about how I could be doing what I really want to do!"

A picture of my future was beginning to form in my mind, and I felt excited by what I saw!

WHEN COURAGE CALLS

What would life be if we had no courage
to attempt anything?
Vincent van Gogh

We live in rattlesnake country, so we are used to staying alert to the reptiles' presence. Many times, they spot us first and hurry away before we even notice them, but if a person happens to startle one or corner it, that's when it's likely to strike.

Generally, we keep our yard cleared of brush and debris that would make good places for snakes to hang out. But we do have a stone retaining wall where they sun themselves sometimes, and we have a woodpile where they like to lie in wait for mice and chipmunks.

On one of the first warm days last spring, my wife Sophie and I were outside, working in the yard. Our almost-three-year-old daughter Charlotte had joined us and was happily trotting around. Also enjoying the sunshine was KeeKee, our calico cat.

We had gotten KeeKee when Charlotte was first starting to say words, and "KeeKee" was her version of "kitty." So KeeKee became our cat's name. Our daughter had spent a lot of time playing with KeeKee, babbling to her, and even dressing the poor kitty up in doll clothes. KeeKee bore all of this with surprising patience and dignity. She and Charlotte seemed quite devoted to each other, and we often found the two of them curled up together, taking a nap.

Now, out in the yard, Charlotte wandered around, chattering and singing to herself. KeeKee meanwhile sprawled in the warm grass, taking a cat nap.

"Stay close to Mommy and Daddy," I told Charlotte.

"Okay," she said.

Sofie and I tried to keep an eye on her, but eventually we got engrossed in digging out some shrubs that had died during the winter, and we forgot to watch our daughter.

The first moment I realized something was wrong was when I heard an angry yowl and caught a glimpse of calico fur flashing across the yard. Then I heard Charlotte scream and burst into tears of fright.

Sophie and I sprinted toward the spot where Charlotte was wailing near the woodpile. Sophie snatched her up and retreated in the direction of the house. I stood, meanwhile, watching in horror as KeeKee whirled in battle with a large diamondback. The growling and hissing were ferocious. Still clutching a shovel, I raised it to strike, but was afraid to do so for fear I might hit KeeKee instead of the snake.

Then suddenly, it was over. The two animals broke apart from each other, and the rattler slipped quickly out of sight.

"KeeKee, are you all right?" I asked, but she was still hissing and growling at the retreating snake. After a moment, though, she turned and started to come toward me, but collapsed in the grass.

"Is Charlotte okay?" I called anxiously over my shoulder.

"She says she's fine," Sophie responded. "She's scared, but she says the snake didn't bite her."

I crouched down by KeeKee, but when I reached out to try to pick her up, she growled at me.

Sophie brought Charlotte closer, but did not put her down. "Tell Daddy what happened," she prompted.

"The snake wanted to bite me," Charlotte said through her tears. "Then KeeKee came and it bit her."

"Bring me a towel or something to wrap KeeKee in," I told Sophie. "She won't let me pick her up."

"Bring me a towel or something to wrap KeeKee in," I told Sophie. "She won't let me pick her up."

Sophie handed Charlotte to me. "Don't put her down," she warned. "KeeKee might bite if she is in pain." Then she ran toward the house.

"Is KeeKee going to die?" Charlotte asked me.

"Don't worry sweetie," I said quickly, brushing the tears off her cheeks. "We'll take her to the kitty hospital, and they'll do all they can to make her all well. Are you sure the snake didn't bite you?" I asked. "Did he even hit you with his head?"

"The snake didn't bite me," Charlotte insisted. "The snake bit KeeKee."

"Okay, just checking," I said, giving her a hug.

Sophie came hurrying back with a box and an old baby blanket of Charlotte's to wrap KeeKee in. I gave the girl back to her mother and knelt down beside KeeKee. By now the cat was panting and acting restless. She protested some when I wrapped her up and put her in the box, but she seemed too weak to attempt to bite me.

"I'll take her to the vet," I said quickly. "You stay here with Charlotte."

"You'll have to go to the emergency clinic," she reminded me, "because it's Saturday afternoon, and our regular vet isn't open. I'll call and tell them you're on the way."

The drive to the emergency clinic was one of the longest half-hours of my life. I talked to KeeKee thanked her for saving Charlotte from harm, and told her to hang in there. Then I prayed for God to heal our brave little kitty.

Dr. Johnson, the emergency vet, was waiting for us. She did a quick exam and pointed out the swollen spot on Kee-Kee's shoulder where the bite had occurred. She told me she would be running several blood tests on KeeKee, checking her blood pressure, and doing an EKG. Then she picked up the box and hurried into the back.

I called Sophie, even though I didn't have much to report yet. "How's Charlotte?" I asked. "Are we totally certain that she wasn't bitten?"

"She's fine," Sophie assured me. "I checked her over thoroughly after you left, then put her down for a nap. I think she was mostly scared. And she is so worried about her kitty."

"We're really lucky," I said. "We could have been sitting in an emergency room with her right now instead of with KeeKee."

"I still can't believe a cat would do something like that," Sophie said. "It's more like the kind of thing you hear about dogs doing."

"I know. I guess it shows how much KeeKee loves Charlotte."

"I think God must have been watching out for our little girl," Sophie said.

"Yeah. I've said a few prayers that He will take care of KeeKee," I told her.

"Me too."

Dr. Johnson came back soon after that to give me a report. "KeeKee's blood pressure is low, and she has a slow clotting time, which is consistent with a bite from a poisonous snake," she said. "We've started her on IV fluids, and we've given her antivenom, pain medication, and antibiotics."

I nodded. My throat felt very tight. "Is she going to be all right?" I asked.

"Yes, I think she will pull through with no problem," Dr. Johnson assured me. "We'd like to keep her here at least overnight so that we can continue the IV fluids. Then we'll send her home with some antibiotics and pain medication for you to continue."

"Oh, thank God!" I said in relief. Then I gave Dr. Johnson more details about how KeeKee had rushed in to save our young daughter from being bitten by the snake.

"That's very impressive!" Dr. Johnson said. "We will make sure we take excellent care of KeeKee. She is already starting to respond to treatment, and I am sure she will continue to improve. I'll call you this evening to give you an update."

"Thank you so much, Dr. Johnson." We shook hands, and I headed out to my car. Before starting the drive home, I called Sophie to tell her the good news.

"It sounds like our prayers have been answered," she said. "I guess that's what they mean when they say that 'God works in mysterious ways.' I am in awe of the love, devotion, and courage He instilled in the little calico cat we are blessed with." Me too. "I'm heading home now. See you soon."

"Drive safely," Sophie said. "I love you."

"Love you, too."

WHAT WE LEARN FROM ANIMALS

All things bright and beautiful,
All creatures great and small,
All things wise and wonderful,
The Lord God made them all.
Cecil Frances Alexander

The soul is the same in all living creatures,
although the body of each is different.
Hippocrates

Until one has loved an animal,
a part of one's soul remains unawakened.
Anatole France

Compassion for animals
is intimately associated
with goodness of character,
and it may be confidently asserted
that he who is cruel to animals
cannot be a good man.
Arthur Schopenhauer

I am in favor of animal rights as well as human rights.
That is the way of a whole human being.
Abraham Lincoln

LISTENING TO HUNCHES

I have studied many philosophers and many cats.
The wisdom of cats is infinitely superior.

Hippolyte Taine

One day our teenaged daughter, Kaitlyn, came home with a big tawny cat.

"Where did you get that?" I asked her. "And more importantly, what do you plan to do with it?"

Kaitlyn had always been the kind of kid who picked up every oddball thing and brought home every stray she came across.

"He's been hanging around at a friend's house for a couple of weeks," Kaitlyn said, "but her family can't keep him, so I brought him home for you and dad."

"What makes you think we want a cat?" I asked, a little annoyed. But I couldn't help petting the cat as he sat there in Kaitlyn's arms, looking docile and contented.

"Well, when I go off to college next month, you two will be here all alone, and the cat can keep you company."

She was right about our impending "empty nest." Kaitlyn was the youngest of our three children. One had married and moved to another city, and the other was in the military, serving abroad.

"I know this will surprise you," I told her, "but your father and I used to live alone before you kids were born, and we got along just fine."

Kaitlyn laughed and put the cat down so he could start exploring. "Maybe so," she admitted, "but now I think you need a cat. I guess you could say it's just sort of a hunch I had. If you decide you don't like having him here, I'll find him another place to live."

When my husband Steve got home from work, he was surprised to learn that our family now included a cat. But we all seemed to like each other, so we adopted the cat and named him Lionel.

From the start, Lionel seemed more bonded with Steve than he was with me. I could tell because he was always sitting on my husband's lap or on top of him in bed. It didn't really bother me that Lionel had turned out to be Steve's cat. I like to see Steve happy, and having the big kitty around obviously made him feel that way.

However, whenever Lionel was sitting with Steve, he exhibited an odd behavior.

He would run his paws down my husband's chest, on the right side. He never did it to Steve's left side, and he never did it to me.

Because we couldn't explain it, we finally just dismissed the behavior as some amusing, quirky thing peculiar to Lionel.

Then one day when I was online, I ran across an article about dogs who could detect cancer, just from some chemical odor that humans could never hope to be able to sniff. I started wondering if cats could do the same, so I did a search and came up with some cases where this had actually happened.

But even the remote idea that Steve might have something wrong with him was so scary that I had to put it out of my mind. Unfortunately, it kept creeping back, especially whenever I noticed Lionel running his paws along my husband's chest.

Finally, one evening I said to Steve, "You know, it turns out that cats can identify cancer and maybe some other diseases, just like dogs can. Do you think Lionel is trying to tell us something?"

"Well, I don't have cancer, if that's what you mean," Steve said flatly. "I quit smoking years ago, and my lungs feel fine."

"I know," I said, "but I don't think it would hurt for you to get some screening done, just to be on the safe side."

"What am I supposed to tell the doctor," Steve asked, "that my cat thinks I have cancer? I'd get laughed out of the office."

"No, but you could tell him that your father died of cancer, and so did your grandmother."

Steve was silent, apparently having no ready response for this.

"Or," I added, "you can just say that your wife is a worrywart, and she won't give you any peace until you get a checkup."

He smiled at that, but he did not agree to go see the doctor. In fact, it took several weeks before Lionel and I finally convinced Steve to make an appointment.

The doctor felt that, given Steve's family history and the fact that he was a former smoker, it would indeed be a good idea for him to have a CAT scan.

"I've already had a CAT scan from Lionel," Steve joked that evening at home. "I don't know why I have to get another one!"

But neither of us was joking a few days later in the oncologist's office. She told us that the scan had revealed a small tumor in Steve's right lung. She went on to say that the tumor was very likely malignant, and that a needle biopsy could be done to confirm that.

"The good news," she added, "is that we seem to have caught it extremely early, before it has had a chance to spread."

I was clutching Steve's hand, feeling as if the ground had just fallen out from under us. I was sure there were questions I should be asking, but I couldn't think what they were.

"What happens next?" Steve said, in a somewhat shaky voice.

"Well, you will probably have a round of chemotherapy to shrink the tumor, and then we will remove it surgically," she told us. "After that, you'll have another round of chemo just to make sure we got rid of all the cancer cells."

So that's how it was. We got through it with a lot of prayer, plus the love and support of our family and friends. And there was Lionel, of course. He was there to comfort me when Steve was in the hospital, and to sit with Steve and purr to him when he came home.

Thinking back on everything that had happened, I decided it was more than just a series of coincidences. God clearly had a hand in it all. Kaitlyn said she had a hunch about Lionel. That must have been how God was trying to get our attention. Happily, it worked, and Lionel made us aware of Steve's cancer long before any symptoms showed up.

On the day I called Kaitlyn to tell her that her dad had been declared cancer-free, I thanked her for listening to that divine hunch. "It may sound strange to say that God used a cat to help save your father's life, but I really believe that's what happened."

"I believe it, too," Kaitlyn said. "God works in wonderful ways to show His love, and I think we have just witnessed that."

LEARNING ACCEPTANCE

It's not what you look at that matters,
it's what you see.
Henry David Thoreau

After our friend Margaret bought a Sphynx kitten, she invited our family to come meet him. So my husband Mark and I, along with our five-year-old son, Jayden, headed over to Margaret's house one evening.

We were met at the door by a very friendly gray-and-white kitten.

"He doesn't have any hair!" exclaimed Jayden. "Did somebody cut it off?"

"No, he was just born that way," Margaret said with a smile. "Sphynx cats are always hairless. If you sit down on the couch, I'll bet he will climb in your lap and let you pet him."

Jayden and I sat down together, and Mark sat in a chair across from us. "That is one weird-looking cat," he said. "Check out those big ears and all those wrinkles!"

Margaret picked the kitten up and placed him in Jayden's lap, but Jayden seemed afraid to touch him. So I reached over and began stroking the kitten myself.

"He's not totally hairless, is he?" I said to Margaret. "He has the softest, downiest short fur! You should pet him Jayden. His skin feels like velvet."

Jayden reached his hand out tentatively to touch the kitten, who started purring and rubbing up against the boy.

"His name is Benjamin," Margaret told Jayden, "and he's five months old. He's very playful."

"He's got so many wrinkles," Jayden said. But he was smiling a bit now, and he giggled when Benjamin head-butted him.

"I think he likes you," I told him.

"Yeah, I think he does," Jayden agreed.

Margaret brought out one of those cat toys on a stick so that Jayden could play with Benjamin. By the time we left to go home, Jayden had totally forgotten that he had been afraid to touch the strange-looking Sphynx kitty when we first arrived.

"I want a Sphynx kitten," Jayden announced, rather predictably, on our way home.

"Well, let's wait until your birthday, and then we'll see," Mark told him. "I think you'll have to settle for a regular cat with fur, though. Sphynx kitties are kind of rare, and that makes them expensive."

Jayden sighed and seemed to mostly resign himself to waiting until his birthday. After that day, he only mentioned the idea of getting a kitten about once a week, and sometimes not even that often.

Then one afternoon when Jayden came home from kindergarten, he started talking excitedly about a new boy in his class. "His name is Liam," he told me, "and he doesn't have any hair, just like Benjamin the cat!"

"He doesn't have any hair?" I asked, realizing with a sinking feeling what that must mean.

"Right," Jayden went on. "His head is totally bald. Some of the kids were afraid to talk to him because he looked funny, but I wasn't. I went up to him and asked if he was born without hair, like Benjamin."

"And what did Liam say?"

"He said he used to have lots of hair, but then he got sick, and the medicine he took made all his hair fall out. But now he's well again, and his hair is going to grow back, and he gets to go to school."

"It was very nice of you to talk to Liam," I said.

"I liked talking to him," Jayden said. "And he's fun to play with, too. I told the other kids that it was okay to play with him, even if he looks sort of different. So then everybody started playing with him."

Tears stung my eyes, and I found it hard to speak, so I just gave my son a big hug.

"I think Liam is going to be my best friend now," Jayden added. "And when I get my kitten, I will let him play with it. Oh, and maybe Liam can go to Margaret's house and play with Benjamin. I think they would really like each other."

"Yes, I think they would," I agreed.

"Mommy, I'm glad I met Benjamin," Jayden concluded, "because that's how I learned that it doesn't really matter what you look like, as long as you're nice inside. That's the most important thing."

WHEN GOD MADE CATS

When God made cats,
he used the graceful
waving of the grass,
The gentle murmur of the river
as its waters pass,
The happy flight of butterflies
that dart among the flowers,
The peaceful, dreamy quality
of quiet nighttime hours.

When God made cats,
he took the warmth
of sunshine in the spring,
The bright and joyful sound of robins
as they chirp and sing,
He added love and faithfulness
through all the nights and days,
And made a creature who is simply
perfect in all ways!

DIARY OF A FOSTER KITTEN

Cats ask plainly for what they want.
Walter Savage Landor

Day 1
Arrived at my foster home. It's scary being in a big, new place, but lots better than the cage I was in at the animal shelter.

Day 2
Got to explore quite a bit of the house. Met the two big cats and two dogs already in residence. We hissed a little, then mostly ignored each other.

Day 5
I'm really getting into this playing thing! It is totally my favorite thing to do. Here are some of the best toys I've found so far: shoelaces, shower curtains, bedspreads, cobwebs, rugs, dog tails, towels, eyeglasses, toilet paper, pencils, and my own adorable feet and tail!

Day 7
I am just so happy to be alive and to be a kitten and to play and eat and sleep all day long. Life is good! I think the grown-up cats here might have forgotten about how much fun life is. Lots of times when I try to get them to play, they growl at me. Same with the dogs.

Day 9

My foster mom says my ears are too big for me, and that my legs and tail are too long for my body. But who cares about that stuff? I think I'm perfect, just the way I am! I'm really smart, too. I figured out how to get on the kitchen counter by climbing up a towel that was hanging on the oven door. And I can get on the dining room table by jumping on one of the chairs first. I guess I'm just a really good problem solver!

Day 10

Know what else I really love? The computer! When my foster mom is using it, I like walking all over the keys. This gets me lots of attention...not necessarily the good kind of attention, but hey, at least I'm not being ignored! Sometimes I sit in my foster mom's lap and watch stuff move around on the computer screen. There's a bug that's shaped like an arrow. I keep trying to catch it, but it always gets away from me. Today, my foster mom showed me a website with pictures of lots of dogs and cats that need homes. She said my picture will be there pretty soon.

Day 12

Guess what! I'm famous now because my picture is on that website I was telling you about. I found out that "foster home," just means "temporary home." I still have to find a "forever home." I was really disappointed. I like it here, and I don't want to go anyplace else. My foster mom said she would like to adopt me, but she can't because she already has too many animals.

Day 14
Today I went with my foster mom to a great big pet store. I saw lots of dogs and people and cats. There were so many smells and so much noise that I was totally overwhelmed! And terrified, too! I had to stay in a little cage on a table where people could walk by and see me. Some of them talked to me, but I didn't know them, so they scared me. When the day was over, my foster mom put me in a different cage in a room with a glass wall, and then she abandoned me there!

Day 22
I'm finally home again after my terrible week at the pet store place. Wow, what an ordeal that was! There were some other kittens there, but they were in other cages, so I couldn't play with any of them. All of us were older kittens that the rescue people call "teenagers." Nobody seems to want to adopt us as long as there are any little baby kittens available. It's really not fair, if you ask me! The baby kittens will soon be five months old just like me.

Day 23
I'm pretty much back into the swing of things here – playing, eating, sleeping. I've decided I don't really want to have to go back to the pet store, so I need to convince my foster mom to adopt me. I'm already turning the charm factor up as high as it will go.

Day 25
At night I snuggle with my foster mom on the bed. Mostly, I sleep on her legs, but if one of the other cats gets there first, I sleep by her side. When I romp and run through the house, my foster mom says it sounds like a herd of antelopes. She thinks this is funny, but I'm not sure why anybody would be amused by having antelopes running through the house.

Day 28
The two adult cats are being nicer to me now. One lets me snuggle with her while she washes my ears. It reminds me of being with my mama when I was a tiny kitten. The other cat will play with me a little bit now, if he's in the right mood. I've been trying to butter up the dogs, but they are only interested in me if they think they can steal my food.

Day 30
The charm campaign continues. I spend a lot of time purring and rubbing against my foster mom's legs. I try to show off all my cute gray-and-white markings, especially the spot under my chin that makes me look like I'm wearing a goatee.

Day 32
I was having a wonderful time shredding toilet paper this morning when my foster mom walked in. She was not amused.

Day 34

Had a little accident while I was exploring today. Somehow a plant fell off the shelf, and the pot broke into a jillion pieces. I tried to play with the pieces, but my foster mom kept shoving me away. Later on, I worked on getting her to forgive me. It was just an accident, after all, and forgiveness is an important lesson for her to learn, just like "enjoy every day" is an important lesson that I'm learning. I'm not sure if the lesson stuck with her or not, though.

Day 35

Oh no. I learned, to my dismay, that I will have to go back to the big pet store to spend another week trying to find a forever home. I think this may be my foster mom's revenge for my breaking her flower pot and shredding the toilet paper.

Day 43

Got back home yesterday. Today is something called Christmas Eve. There is a big tree in the living room. So much fun to climb on! There are boxes under the tree with paper and ribbon. I can't help myself – I have to play with everything!

Day 44

My foster mom told me she had a special Christmas present for me. She said she has decided to adopt me! I can't believe it – especially after I climbed the tree and knocked some things off of it. I guess my new mom finally learned what I've been trying to teach her all along: Life is full of happy blessings if you just love and forgive!

PROVERBS:
WHAT OUR ANCESTORS
LEARNED FROM CATS

Happy is the home with at least one cat.

The dog may be wonderful prose, but only the cat is poetry.

Nature breaks through the eyes of the cat.

It is better to feed one cat than many mice.

The cat has nine lives—
three for playing,
three for straying,
and three for staying.

No heaven will not ever Heaven be;
unless my cats are there to welcome me.

KITTEN LOVE

I love you, little kitten,
I love your fur so fine.
You give the best of hugs--
That's why I'm glad you're mine!

You purr so very sweetly,
You fill my life with love,
Just like the love that comes
From our Father up above!

HELPING OUT

The cat has too much spirit to have no heart.
Ernest Menaul

When Millie, our cherished Yorkshire Terrier, had her first litter of puppies, I was ecstatic. Millie was a very sweet little dog, and I knew she would be a wonderful mother.

A few years before that, my husband Ken and I, along with our daughter Emma, had moved to an old farmhouse on a small acreage. We didn't do any farming, but we loved being in the country and exploring our pastures. Of course Millie and her pups would be staying in a warm box in our big kitchen for a while.

The time finally came, and Millie gave birth to her tiny, adorable golden and black babies. Just as I expected, she took to being a mother immediately.

Our lives turned upside down, though, when the pups were just a week old. I had put Millie's dinner in her bowl, and she didn't come scampering in to the sound, as she usually did. I went to the make-shift whelping box we had made. And saw only the little pups crawling over one another. No Millie. The search ended in the most heartbreaking way imaginable. I found Millie in the laundry room, lying near a pile of towels. In my heart, I knew something was wrong right away, but I just couldn't wrap my brain around the idea. There had been no clue, no sign at all, that Millie was sick. But she was lifeless. In the coming weeks, we would have to struggle with the news from the vet that she had apparently had an undiognosed heart condition.

Our whole family felt devastated by Millie's death. And to make matters worse, I now had four tiny puppies who would have to be fed by hand for the next two or three weeks. That would mean letting them nurse from a bottle every two hours or so during the day, and at least once during the night.

I had a day job, and so did Ken. Neither one of us had a boss who would approve of our bringing a litter of whining puppies to the office. Emma was in the third grade, so she would be at school and couldn't do the daytime feedings either. None of us could afford to take several weeks off to puppy-sit.

I didn't have another mama dog to take over feeding Millie's pups, and knew of no one who had spoken of a dog having pups recently.

"I just don't know what to do!" I admitted to Ken and Emma. I was crying, of course. I had been sobbing, off and on, all evening. It was past Emma's bedtime, and I should have long since made her go to her room, but I figured she was getting old enough to share in the sad times of family life as well as the happy times.

In the end, it's a good thing I didn't send Emma to bed, because she's the one who came up with the solution to our problem.

"I know!" she exclaimed, "Daisy Mae can nurse the puppies!"

"Daisy Mae?" I said in surprise. "Daisy Mae is a cat!"

"Of course she's a cat," Emma said, in that matter-of-fact way of 8-year-olds. "But ever since we gave away her last kitten yesterday, she has been feeling depressed. I think she would like a new family of puppies to adopt."

Daisy Mae was one of our barn cats. We had been so happy to have found homes for all her four-week-old kittens, but I had indeed seen her earlier in the day, wandering around, meowing, as if she were still looking for them.

Ken was laughing. "A cat nursing puppies! Now there's something I'd like to see!"

"Emma," I said, "I just don't think it's going to work. A cat won't adopt puppies."

"I think she will," Emma insisted. "I saw a picture on the internet of a mama cat nursing puppies. And I think Daisy Mae will want to help us out because she loves us."

"I'll go out and try to find Daisy Mae," Ken said.

"Well, I've never heard of such a thing being done," I said, "but I guess it wouldn't hurt to try it. The worst that will happen is that Daisy Mae will just walk away from the puppies. And if we're going to try it, we should probably do it now," I added. "Those babies sound like they're getting pretty hungry."

"Take a dish of tuna with you," I said. "That should help."

About ten minutes later, Ken was back, toting a gray tabby under one arm. He set her down, and she immediately began to explore the kitchen. I was pretty sure she had only been in the house once or twice, so this was a new adventure for her.

"Hi, Daisy Mae," Emma said, stroking the cat. "Do you want to meet Millie's puppies?"

Daisy Mae pretty much ignored Emma and continued snooping around, but when she came to the whelping box, she paused and thrust her head inside. Daisy Mae seemed curious, but wary! The pups were really beginning to cry now, and I started wondering if I had any puppy milk substitute formula on hand.

Then, to my amazement, Daisy Mae jumped into the box with the puppies and began to nuzzle and groom them. After a few moments, she stretched out on her side. The pups must have been able to smell quite clearly that this was not their mama Millie. But the invitation to nurse apparently is the same in any language. Soon the sound of contented puppies filled the kitchen.

I gave a sigh of relief and smiled at Emma and Ken.

Well, you certainly taught us something tonight," I said to my daughter.

She shook her head. "No, I think Daisy Mae was the teacher. She showed us that if you know a way to help somebody out, you should just do it. That's the lesson."

"That's an excellent lesson," said Ken. And he gave Emma a big hug.

THE NATURE OF CATS

When a cat flatters ... he is not insincere:
you may safely take it for real kindness.
Walter Savage Landor

It is impossible for a lover of cats
to banish these alert, gentle,
and discriminating little friends,
who give us just enough
of their regard and complaisance
to make us hunger for more.
Agnes Repplier

All cats love fish but fear to wet their paws.
Proverb

After dark, all cats are leopards.
Proverb

A man who carries a cat by the tail learns
something he can learn in no other way.
Mark Twain

I like cats.... When I meet a cat,
I say, 'Poor Pussy!' and stoop down
and tickle the side of its head;
and the cat sticks up its tail
in a rigid, cast-iron manner,
arches its back, and wipes its nose
up against my trousers;
and all is gentleness and peace.
Jerome K. Jerome

THE CAT AND THE VACUUM

Don't tell God how big the storm is.
Tell the storm how big your God is.

It's the vacuum cleaner that worries Sally's cat, Feathers.
Sally believes that Feathers' fear of the vacuum began the
day Sally pushed the roaring machine into a walk-in closet
where, unknown to her, Feathers was sleeping. The next
thing she knew, a cat with her long fur standing on end and
saucer-sized eyes blazing zoomed passed her, out the closet,
and disappeared.

Several hours of vacuum-free silence reigned over the
house before Feathers cautiously emerged from her hiding
place. The cat stuck close to the walls, eyeing available
means of escape, until she assured herself the vacuum was
safely contained.

Now, years later, Feathers goes into hiding whenever Sally
brings out the vacuum—the cat doesn't even wait for her to
turn it on. Even if Sally's cleaning takes her nowhere near
the cat's current resting spot, Feathers takes cover someplace
out of sight.

Many times, however, where Feathers chooses to hide is
right where Sally intends to vacuum, and so begins Feathers'

run from room to room, each time followed in several minutes by Sally and the fearsome beast.

"She gets more and more agitated," Sally reported. "I wish I could tell her that the walk-in closet 'attack' was a mistake—it won't happen again!" But according to Feathers, it could...and she doesn't want to be around if it does.

When I think of Feathers and her fear of the vacuum, it reminds me of times I'm afraid to attempt something because I tried it once, and it failed...or backfired...or flopped completely. Rather than look at the specific circumstances and examine what I did and what I could do differently, I decide—like Feathers—to distance myself from the whole thing. Just not go there.

I have to remind myself that one bad encounter doesn't mean I had a run-in with a malicious beast out to get me. It just means I've learned a lesson...and that's a good thing. When I go for it again, perhaps the "beast" won't look so beastly after all...or maybe might be afraid of me!

KITTY'S BEDTIME PRAYER

Now I lay me down to sleep,
I pray this cushy life to keep.
I pray for toys that look like mice,
and sofa cushions, soft and nice.
For grocery bags where I can hide,
just like a tiger, crouched inside!
I pray for gourmet Kitty snacks,
and someone nice to scratch my back.
For window sills all warm and bright,
for shadows to explore at night.
I pray I'll always stay real cool,
and keep the secret feline rule
To Never tell a human that...
the world is really ruled by CATS!
Author Unknown